NAZIS of LONG ISLAND

SEDITION, ESPIONAGE & THE PLOT AGAINST AMERICA

CHRISTOPHER C. VERGA

Foreword by Karl Grossman

THE History PRESS

Published by The History Press
An imprint of Arcadia Publishing
Charleston, SC
www.historypress.com

Front cover: Bungalow in Camp Siegfried, Yaphank. *Courtesy of the Longwood Library, Bayles Local History Room and Photograph Archives. Back cover*: During the annual German Day rally inside Camp Siegfried in Yaphank. *Courtesy of the Longwood Library, Bayles Local History Room and Photograph Archives.*

First published 2025

Manufactured in the United States

ISBN 9781467156493

Library of Congress Control Number: 2025941130

Notice: The information in this book is true and complete to the best of our knowledge. It is offered without guarantee on the part of the author or The History Press. The author and The History Press disclaim all liability in connection with the use of this book.

CONTENTS

ACKNOWLEDGEMENTS

No one person can own or monopolize the history they write or interpret. The gatekeeper to our history lies in the collective efforts of a community to preserve it. Whoever we recognize as a hero or a villain is defined by the impact they have on the communities they represent. World War II–era Long Island had a complex history. The war was fought on many fronts: domestic, foreign and the overlooked front of public opinion. World War II was a total war in which every aspect of society contributed to the war effort. Morale throughout all towns and counties was crucial in manufacturing fighter planes and armor. Subversive groups funded by enemy governments attacked morale and public trust in our democratic institutions, but collectively, America withstood all such attacks. This story is preserved in the archives of many town and county historical societies and local libraries. Through the collective efforts of these agencies, the legacy of endurance will be preserved for future generations.

This book would not have been possible without the help and support of the many people who tirelessly work to preserve this history through image collections and interviews. The Smithtown Library's Veterans Oral History Project played a crucial role in re-creating veterans' experiences before the war. I would like to thank Paul Infranco and Melanie Cardone-Leather of the Longwood Public Library for the images and background information they provided on Camp Siegfried and Camp Upton. I want to express my gratitude for the photos and access to the internment camp letters offered to me by Dr. Geri Solomon and Hofstra University's Special

Collections. These images and documents were the backbone of retelling an almost forgotten history. I want to extend special recognition to all the local historians I consulted with at the Bay Shore and Nassau County Historical Societies. I want to thank Marvin Miller, author of *Wunderlich's Salute: The Interrelationship of the German American Bund, Camp Siegfried, Yaphank, Long Island, and the Young Siegfrieds*. Your book, written over forty years ago, still shocks and surprises Long Islanders with the treason and sedition organized at Camp Siegfried. I want to thank the talented Nino Siragusa, who convinced me to update my professional headshot by providing an amazing alternative.

I want to thank Jill Santiago and Suffolk Community College's Center for Social Justice and Human Understanding. The work of the center retells the atrocities of the Holocaust to demonstrate that hate has no place in our society.

Most of all, I would like to thank all who fought against the rising tide of fascism, foreign and domestic. This book is an attempt to honor and preserve your efforts for future generations. With collective efforts to protect our democracy, we will prevent those who died in service to their country from dying a second death: being forgotten.

FOREWORD

Nazis of Long Island: Sedition, Espionage & the Plot Against America is a book about the American Nazi movement and the strong resistance to curtailing its spread.

This is a story that reverberates with similarities today. A resurgence of Nazism and fascism, so-called neo-Nazism and neofascism, has been and is going on worldwide. Has it been the beginning of history repeating itself? The playwright Eugene O'Neill had a character in his 1947 play *A Moon for the Misbegotten* declare: "There is no present or future—only the past happening over and over again—now." If we are to avoid the horrendous, deadly events of less than a century ago, we need to learn fully about what happened then.

Historically, Long Island was a "Breeding Ground for an American Reich," as Christopher Verga has titled his second chapter. What made the region vulnerable to this ideology was the long-standing influence of the Ku Klux Klan, with pro-Klan candidates in positions in local and county governments. Combined with influence from Depression-era European fascist movements and a dose of far-right radio commentary, the biggest other threat was the growing belief that democracy was dead. An interconnected U.S. network of Nazi indoctrination camps further deepened a more significant anti-government Nazi movement called the German American Bund. Facing Nazi rallies, brave grassroots organizations and public officials fought tirelessly. Ultimately, it took a world war and many millions of deaths to destroy Nazism.

In January 2024, German Chancellor Olaf Scholz, as reported by Reuters, "voiced concern over the rise of extreme-right tendencies in his country 79 years after the Auschwitz extermination camp was liberated." Scholz said, "New reports are emerging all the time: about neo-Nazis and their dark networks." And it's not just Germany in which neo-Nazis are active. It's a global situation, with neo-Nazi activity in many countries.

In the United States, there has been a Nazi resurgence. The headline of a 2021 op-ed in the *Los Angeles Times* by Martin Puchner, a professor of English and comparative literature at Harvard University, was: "I Thought I'd Escaped Germany's Dark History. The Capitol Attack Reminded Me I Was Wrong." Puchner wrote:

> *When I came to America a quarter of a century ago, I was leaving behind history's No. 1 villain. True, Germany had grappled with its crimes, belatedly, in the 1980s by teaching the horrors of the Third Reich in high schools. But the burden of the past lingered, and I was glad to escape it. At least that's what I thought I was doing until a string of events that began with right-wing vigilantes waving Nazi flags in Charlottesville, Va., and ended with an attack on the Capitol....*
>
> *Are we reliving the 1920s, when deeply divided Germany saw the erosion of democratic institutions, a police force sympathetic to the right, and the rise of a politician who used a new media technology, the radio, to reach a growing audience? Are we in the early 1930s, when a delegitimized election process, fed off years of economic depression and an assault on parliament, led to the suspension of democracy? When seen through a German lens, history isn't repeating itself so much as darting back and forth, a messy jumble in which America seems to be reliving German 20th-century history at once.*

The Southern Poverty Law Center, in its online information sheet titled "Neo-Nazi," starts by saying, "After several years of struggling to hold mass in-person events, the neo-Nazi movement managed to regain some of its organizational footing in 2023." It cites fifty members of several groups gathering for a demonstration in Orlando, Florida, billed as "March of the Red Shirts." Although this "brought an unprecedented number of neo-Nazi activists together for the first time, it followed on the heels of similar, albeit smaller, flash demonstrations organized by neo-Nazi activists in Ohio, Texas, Wisconsin, Florida, Massachusetts, Maine, and Tennessee." Instead of public schools combating this indifference by teaching the rise of intolerance as a cautionary tale, the group Moms for Liberty has been taking over school boards throughout the country, demanding bans on teaching anything related to critical race theory and LGBTQ+ themes. Leaders of Moms for Liberty, in their public statements and their newsletter, *The Parent Brigade*, have used a famous quote by Hitler—"He alone, who owns youth, gains the future"—to justify their national book-banning campaigns.

In this book, Verga provides a history of what the Nazis did decades ago and what was done and not done to halt them. We need to learn from the history detailed by Verga to help guide us in what we can and must do now to avoid tragedy in our time.

Karl Grossman
Professor of Journalism
State University of New York at Old Westbury

CHAPTER 1

NAZI INVASION OR AN INVITE TO COME IN

Around midnight on June 13, 1942, a dense fog rolled in off the shore of Amagansett, New York. Twenty-one-year-old Coast Guardsman Jack Cullen was conducting his assigned six-mile patrol along the beach. In the distance, a rubber raft struggled to fight the rough surf through the thick fog. When they reached the shore, four men in swimsuits were carrying canvas seabags.

Cullen, witnessing the landing of the raft, called out from a distance, "What's the trouble?" The four men did not respond and walked toward Cullen. Unarmed and scared, Cullen, in a loud, assertive tone, yelled, "Who are you?" and reached for his flashlight at his hip. One of the four men, thinking Cullen was reaching for a gun, cried out, "Wait a minute. Are you the Coast Guard?"[1] Cullen told them, "I am," and the same man replied, "We are a couple of fishermen from Southampton who ran aground." Cullen instructed the men to return to the station until daybreak. In rebuttal to the offer, the spokesperson of the so-called stranded fishermen said, "Wait a minute—you don't know what's going on. How old are you? Do you have a father and a mother? I wouldn't want to have to kill you." As the spokesperson for the four men addressed Cullen, another of the men, who spoke German, dragged more seabags to shore. Cullen then asked, "What is in the bag?" The spokesman for the four told him, "Clams," and then said calmly, "Forget this whole thing happened," and handed him $100. Cullen started to say, "I don't want it," but he was cut off in mid-sentence by the spokesman: "Then take $300." The man then told Cullen, "Look me in the eye. Would you recognize me again if you saw me in East Hampton?" Cullen said, "No. I have never seen you in my life."[2] The spokesperson for the men then told Cullen, "My name is J.W. Davis."

Cullen told the man his name and calmly walked down the beach. As Cullen lost sight of the four men in the fog, he began to run back to the station. Once back at the station, Cullen reported the event to commanding officer Carl Ross Jenette, who organized a search team of armed guardsmen to detain the suspicious men. As the search team descended along the shore, the four men changed their clothes and buried their seabags containing some of the $175,000 in cash (approximately $3 million in today's dollars), wooden crates of explosives and maps in a nearby dune. Walking half a mile through the shadows of the fog, the men approached ticket window clerk Ira Baker at the Amagansett train station. The spokesman for the men asked for four one-way tickets to Jamaica station and said, "The fishing hasn't been very good out here. In fact, it's very miserable because of the fog, and I guess we'll go home."

The spokesman was named George Dasch, and his three colleagues were Ernest Burger, Robert Quirin and Heinrich Heinck. All four men were part of one of two teams sent to commit large-scale attacks of sabotage on American infrastructure. In Germany, the two teams of four were trained by the Abwehr (Nazi military intelligence) and by the Nazi high command for a commando-style raid. All four men had lived in or visited America before the war and had a basic understanding of transportation lines and local communities. All four men were directly or indirectly affiliated with the German American Bund's Midwest and New York chapters. The code name given to the operation was Pastorius. Nazi high command selected this name after German-born pioneer Francis Daniel Pastorius, who founded the first German settlement in America, named Germantown, in 1683, in what is now Pennsylvania. During training, the commanders compared how Daniel Pastorius faced the unknown in America but succeeded in doing so—and how they, too, would face uncertainty in achieving success. (What the Nazi propagandist left out of the narrative of Pastorius was that he was a pioneer in American democracy. Once he established his settlement, he criticized absolutism, set up elected positions and took a strong antislavery stance.) Ernest Burger was one of the two men in the group of four to have received United States military training and one of the two in the operation to have U.S. citizenship. Burger held the rank of private through his service in the Michigan National Guard.

Dasch was a New York City and Philadelphia resident who served in the United States Army Air Corps and the United States Army First Infantry

Division, Twenty-Eighth Regiment. The landing site of Long Island was chosen because Dasch once stayed on the island and was familiar with its parkways, transit lines and some of its communities. Heinrich Heinck was a one-time resident of the Bronx and served in a leadership role in the Bronx unit of the German American Bund. Heinrich returned to Germany in 1939 after being recruited by the German Labor Front for the Heim ins Reich campaign (German Aryans returning to Germany to help in the war effort). Richard Quirin lived in New York City and was a member of the Bund with the rank of Ordnungsdienst (the Ordnungsdienst was part of the Bund's paramilitary unit). Ernest Kuber was initially assigned to the Long Island team but did not receive final departure orders. Kuber was a one-time resident of New York City and an active Bund member who was deported back to Germany.

Before the men embarked from Germany, they were given suitcases with false bottoms to store cash, guns, money belts and handkerchiefs with the contact information of Captain William Drechsel of New Jersey, Carl Krepper of Newark, New Jersey, and Walter Froehling of Chicago. This information would become visible only when the handkerchiefs were treated with ammonia fumes.

The primary contact, William Drechsel, was familiar with the waterfront because he navigated German cruise liners such as the SS *Bremen* for the North Deutsches Lloyd Ship Company, which docked in New York harbors. According to U.S. Navy intel, Drechsel was a member of the Nazi Party and a former U-boat captain during World War I. Relocating to the United States did not change his loyalty to Germany, which made the FBI suspect him of providing intelligence about U.S. docks to the Nazi navy and potentially manufacturing speedboats for the saboteurs to make planned escapes once they carried out their missions along the waterfront. Carl Krepper was an active Bund and German American Business League member who offered to provide a safe house and identification papers for the men while they were in the Greater New York area. Froehling was the uncle of Herbert Haupt (a member of the second sabotage team to land in Florida) and an active Bund member who assisted the second sabotage team with building a network of sympathizers. Froehling and his wife, Lucille, were also assigned to store explosives for the men. For their service to the Nazi government, Walter Froehling and his wife received $10,000. Midwest Bund member Otto Wergin and his wife, Kate, worked with the Froehlings to provide additional support. Wergin's son, Wolfgang, was Herbert Haupt's close friend. Wolfgang and Herbert both left America for Germany in 1940 to serve the Nazi government. Wolfgang would join the Wehrmacht and be sent to the Eastern Front. Herbert Haupt's parents, Hans and Erna Haupt, would provide support for the second team. The Haupts, like all the other network members, were affiliated with the Bund, and they were assigned to the second team once they arrived in Chicago.

The two teams of four men were ordered by the Nazi high command to blow up selected targets that would create mass panic. The New York team was assigned to blow up the New York City power grid, the Hell Gate Bridge and critical parts of the Pennsylvania Railroad terminal. Walter Kappe, a former Bund leader and a frequent visitor to Camp Siegfried in Yaphank, Long Island, moved to Germany and joined the Nazi Abwehr. Due to his knowledge of New York, he was assigned to select all the New York targets. Before taking over the sabotage operation, Kappe specialized in English radio propaganda, but he soon moved up the ranks to supervise and plan various clandestine missions. Before the two teams set out, Kappe supplied all the men with well-forged Social Security cards, draft registration cards reflecting draft exceptions and maps of targeted destinations and escape routes. Both teams would sail on a two-week voyage from France with a U-boat crew of fourteen men. When the teams arrived, they would be sent from the sub to an inflatable boat with a few wooden crates containing explosives and seabags containing material to help them navigate their assigned city of operations.

As planned, the four men in New York would take a train to Jamaica, Queens. Once in Queens, they would purchase a change of clothes, break off into two groups and take the train into Manhattan. Dasch and Burger had reservations about the operation and planned to defect once they landed. During his training, Burger noticed Dasch's difficulty and unease in carrying out orders and standing at attention to "Heil Hitler."[3] These observations made Burger believe that Dasch was like-minded in his assessments of the Nazi control of Europe, and Burger confided in Dasch about his discontent. Both men were looking to escape Germany due to their negative interactions with the Gestapo and the eroding economic conditions. Before departing Germany, Kappe told Burger, "You have been in the hands of the Gestapo for a while, but I have confidence in your rehabilitation." Burger interpreted this statement as meaning agents in New York City would watch him on his arrival.

As planned, once in New York City, Dasch, Burger, Heinck and Quirin broke off into two teams of two. Knowing that there could be Gestapo agents in the city watching FBI offices, Dasch first called the FBI office to turn himself in and to inform agents of the saboteurs' plans. After the call, Dasch arranged to meet agents in person at the FBI's Washington, D.C., offices. Burger and Dasch got rooms at the Governor Clinton Hotel, and Heinck and Quirin at the Chesterfield Hotel, per their instructions from Berlin. In the morning, they met at Grant's Tomb in Harlem to discuss the next steps in the plan.

Heinck and Quirin proposed hiding within the German communities in New York to evade the authorities until they could take a train to Chicago. Dasch and Burger disagreed and said they would stay at the hotel. All four would remain at the Clinton Hotel on their last night in NYC. Earlier in the evening, Dasch left the Clinton and gave a note to the reception desk to deliver to Burger. The note stated he was going to D.C. to meet with FBI agents. Burger carelessly stored the note in a drawer within the room. Quirin stayed in Burger's room before departing in the morning, which was not part of the plan. While Burger was asleep, Quirin found Dasch's note and alerted Heinck, who had taken the next train out of New York City. Heinck contacted his friends Herman and Hildegarde Faje to ask for help storing money for the mission. Heinck promised Herman that he would be awarded an Iron Cross Second Class if he assisted. Herman agreed to hide Heinck's money belt containing $3,600 in the radiator in his house.

Delaying his arrival for a few days, Dasch checked in at the Mayflower Hotel in Washington, D.C., on June 25. Once checked in, he contacted FBI agents Duane Traynor and Frank Johnstone using his assumed code name, David Pastorius. To validate his story about the plot, he turned over a briefcase containing $80,000 to the agents and stated that the money was given to him by Lieutenant Kappe, who was part of the German high command.[4] In further statements, Dasch told agents, "I have a mission coming here—to fight Hitler. One part is defensive in locating the men attempting to blow up the commercial industry targets. I could not fight Hitler in Germany, but I can fight him here through propaganda. I want to communicate my story to the German people through the radio."[5] When asked about additional material and information he might have, Dasch stated he had a personal notebook containing names and notes, but lost it when landing on the beach.

On June 27, Dasch met with the federal district attorney's office to discuss his potential testimony. During the discussion, Dasch expressed concern about his family in Germany and that his eyewitness account in open court could endanger them. The district attorney's office proposed that he plead guilty and be sentenced. Once he was committed to prison, the FBI would recommend that he receive a presidential pardon for his cooperation. Although he was initially in support of the plan, Dasch would change his mind and plead innocent, arguing that he never intended to come to America to commit sabotage.

Soon after Dasch turned himself in, Burger was arrested at the Clinton Hotel. After his arrest, he confirmed Dasch's story. After landing on the beach, Burger further described how he did not attempt to bury or conceal the items they brought, despite being instructed to do so. After being seen by the Coast Guard, Burger assumed they would be caught anyway. During a later search of the beach, Burger's personal effects and German-issued uniform were found lying out in the open on the beach.

Abwehr commander Kappe had a lesser role in organizing the second team sent to Florida. Landing twenty miles from Jacksonville, the team was assigned to targets in the Chicago area. The four men on the Florida team were Edward Kerling, Hermann Neubauer, Werner Thiel and Herbert Haupt. Before relocating to Germany, Kerling, the Florida team leader, lived in New York City and was the only team member with an active membership in the Queens, New York, Bund. Kerling is believed to have participated in one of the many rallies at Camp Siegfreid in Yaphank. Kerling's active Bund membership gave him multiple contacts for potential safe houses throughout New York City. Neubauer was a one-time Chicago and Florida resident and a former Midwest Bund member. During federal investigations into the Bund in late 1939, all noncitizens, including Neubauer, were asked to resign in order to distance themselves from Germany's increasing global hostilities. Neubauer then joined the Bund's local affiliated group, Deutscher Volksbund. Werner Thiel immigrated to the United States in 1927 and worked various jobs in Jersey City. By the mid-1930s, Thiel had moved to New York City and worked as a laborer until he returned to Germany in 1941. Herbert Haupt, the youngest of the four men and the only American citizen, would attempt to desert the team by the end of the week.

Before landing, there was a discussion among the four about the likelihood of success. Kerling, on the sub, refrained from expressing his doubts about the mission and disregarded team members' concerns. After landing, Kerling contacted Bund member Helmut Leiner of Astoria, Queens. Leiner was tasked with providing Kerling with the contact information of other Nazi sympathizers in the Midwest. The assigned bases of their operations would be in Chicago and Cincinnati. Kerling and Neubauer stayed together and checked in at the Seminole Hotel in the center of Jacksonville under the assumed names of Nicolas and Kelly. Before the group split up and

Kerling went to the hotel, he told Thiel he would not carry out the mission and expressed doubt about the mission's success. Neubauer later testified, "Kerling was nervous and did not want to get into the taxicab to go to the hotel." But Kerling described Neubauer as unable to sleep and jumpy after checking in at the hotel.

Thiel and Haupt stayed at another hotel nearby and, in the morning, took the first train to Chicago (they were supposed to go to Cincinnati). Once they reached Chicago, Haupt contacted Froehling. Froehling contacted Haupt's parents, who lived in Chicago, and invited them over to meet with their son. After Haupt explained his mission to his parents, he departed Froehling's home and spent the night at his childhood home. Before leaving for the night, Haupt told Froehling that the other three would contact him at his house around one o'clock on Sunday afternoon. In the meantime, Haupt, without telling the other team members, would take the money allotted for the mission to buy his father a car the following day. But Haupt had additional plans that differed from the mission. He had been in a relationship with Chicago native Gerda Melind before returning to Germany for training. After the night at his parents' house, Haupt asked Melind to marry him, and she accepted.[6] He then changed his name to Larry Jordan, registered with the Selective Service the following week, applied for work at the Simpson Optical Company and tried to get lost in the backdrop of Chicago.

The remaining three team members attempted to contact Froehling, who was directed to provide material support and set up additional meetings between the saboteurs. Neubauer, while regrouping, contacted his friends, Harry and Emma Jaques. Meeting them at their home, Neubauer asked them to hide $3,600 for him, explaining he was on a secret mission. Neubauer was vague in his explanation and withheld the details of the mission.

With their explosives, Kerling, Neubauer and Thiel headed to New York. While in New York City, Kerling met with Helmut Leiner at Grand Central Station. During their conversation, Leiner later stated, he told Kerling about alien travel regulations and gasoline rationing. After Kerling and Leiner's meeting, all three team members checked into the Knickerbocker Hotel to await further instructions. Leiner contacted Kerling's estranged wife, Maria, and asked her to go on a blind date. When she refused, Leiner told her the blind date was with her husband, Kerling. Maria agreed to meet with Leiner and Kerling in Central Park, but Kerling would be detained before the meeting. Before the proposed meeting, Thiel and Kerling contacted one-time Friends of New Germany and Bund member Anthony Cramer. The men arranged their last meeting, hoping to get a safe place to lie low and stash their effects.

Dasch's and Burger's statements to the FBI were key to the arrests of all four members of the Florida team and, later, the remaining members of the New York team. Kerling was arrested in front of the Shelton Hotel on Lexington Avenue in New York City by FBI Agent Thomas Donegan. In custody, Kerling demanded his "civil rights" and claimed his rights were violated because Donegan hit him in the face during his arrest and interrogation. After the complaint, agents allowed Donegan to take Kerling into another room for a few minutes. On his return, Kerling retracted his statement and said, "Well, agent Donegan brushed me lightly on my face." When Kerling asked for a lawyer, the agents told him he would be provided one at the right time. (The right to a lawyer during interrogation did not extend to enemy combatant cases or non-civilian courts.) Searching Kerling's personal effects, agents found random slips of paper with addresses on them. When asked, Kerling disclosed that those were the addresses where his colleagues could be located.

Once all the men from both teams were in custody, they all claimed they were trying to escape the oppression of the Reich. Before their mission, the detainees did not expect charges to be levied against them or a trial; they thought they would be detained as POWs. United States Attorney General Francis Biddle filed four charges against the saboteurs: violation of the law of war (as they were agents of an enemy nation secretly dressed in civilian clothes to carry out a military operation), violation of the Eighty-First Article of War (conspiracy to dress as civilians to commit acts of espionage or sabotage), violation of the Eighty-Second Article of War (sedition or desertion to an enemy) and criminal conspiracy to commit acts of sabotage. A civilian trial lacked legal precedent, and the men were sent to a military tribunal. President Roosevelt personally selected the seven tribunal members: Major General Frank McCoy, Major General Walter Grant, Major General Blanton Winship, Major General Lorenzo Gasser, Brigadier General Guy Henry, Brigadier General John Lewis and Brigadier General John T. Kennedy. The two defense lawyers appointed were Colonel Cassius Dowell and Colonel Kenneth Royall. One of the questions before the tribunal was whether to file charges against Burger and Dasch. Captain Lyle Keith, the prosecutor, focused on making all four charges stick and argued that there should be no leniency toward Burger and Dasch. In a written argument to the court, Captain Keith stated, "Dasch decided not to become a naturalized citizen while in America and put a lot of effort into returning to Germany in 1941. Burger was a member of Hitler's National Socialist Party before coming to America and on his return to Germany. This does not reflect any intention for either of them to stay in America."

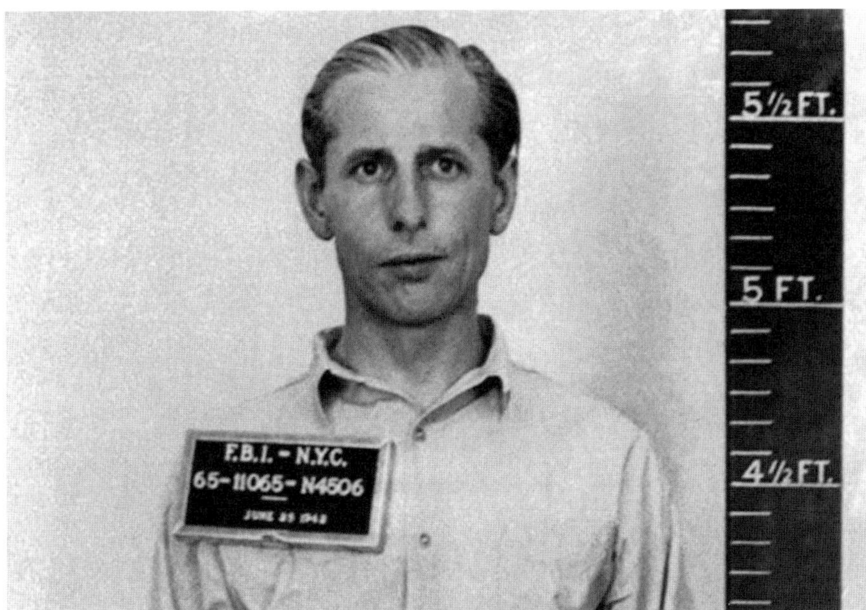

George Dasch, one of the two members of Operation Pastorius who turned themselves in and cooperated with the FBI. *Library of Congress.*

Captain Keith further argued in his written statement to the court:

> *Dasch's statement was inconsistent; both men took pains in concealing their identity, and neither relinquished control of the explosives they brought nor spoke to the other men about withdrawing from the conspiracy. They took meticulous care to continue in the conspiracy until they felt it was the opportune moment to reveal their identity and the purpose of the trip. I have a relatively strong feeling that, at least so far as Dasch is concerned, and possibly the same observation applies to Burger, no intention to withdraw from the group's activities ever came into existence until fear began to reach into their hearts. Neither took a single step to make their activities known to this government until the Coast Guard discovered their landing. Dasch lost his notebook with the addresses of all additional collaborating members who could identify them. So far as Burger is concerned, and his story to the effect that he probably dropped and did not conceal items on the beach to make sure that they would be discovered, it is rather difficult to become convinced of the truthfulness of that statement. It seems far more reasonable that the articles dropped by Burger were dropped as a result of excitement rather than as an effort on his part to lead American officials to them.*[7]

The next challenge for the prosecution was that the two U.S. citizens, Herbert Haupt and Ernest Burger, both had a legal claim against being tried as enemy combatants. Biddle denaturalized the two based on their transfer of allegiance to Nazi Germany, making them enemy aliens and subject to court-martial. Despite all legal arguments, the sentences would carry the death penalty for all eight men.

The fourteen civilians who aided the eight saboteurs were tried in civilian court. Herman and Hildegarde Faje were charged with treason and were both held as enemy aliens until their January 1946 trial. Charges against Hildegarde were later dropped, but Herman was sentenced to five years in prison. Drechsel, not one of the fourteen indicted on charges of aiding the saboteurs, was implicated in testimony but was never fully connected to the plot. Drechsel would later be connected to various Nazi spy rings and charged with not registering as a foreign agent. He would be stripped of his citizenship and sentenced to eighteen months in prison for his conviction.

Six of the fourteen defendants in Chicago, Hans and Erna Haupt, Walter and Lucille Froehling and Otto and Kate Wergin, were found guilty of treason on November 14, 1942. Before handing down the sentences, Judge William Campbell told the six:

> *How different was this trial from the treatment given in Germany to a person accused of a similar offense against the German Reich? The home front is our titanic struggle against the enemy, equally important and certainly more vulnerable than our battle lines. To endanger this home front, therefore, is as treasonable as spiking our guns in the face of the foe.*

Hans, Walter and Otto were initially sentenced to death, and their wives, Erna, Lucille and Kate, were sentenced to twenty-five years. The sentences and convictions were overturned on appeal because the confessions were in violation of the defendants' Sixth Amendment right to counsel. Otto and Walter were indicted on the lesser charge of concealment of knowledge of treason and served five years. Hans was tried and convicted a second time of treason and received a life sentence, but was granted amnesty by President Eisenhower in 1957. Helmut Leiner was indicted on charges of treason, and Maria Kerling and her boyfriend, Ernest Herman Kerkhof, were indicted for concealment of knowledge of treason. Kerkhof and Maria had all charges against them dropped but were detained as enemy aliens throughout the war. Leiner was acquitted but had charges refiled against him. Leiner pleaded guilty to trading with the enemy and received a sentence of eighteen

An eleven-man military commission overseeing the trial of the eight Nazi saboteurs at the Department of Justice building in July 1942. Sitting on the commission (*left to right*) are Brigadier General John T. Lewis; Major General Lorenzo D. Casser; Major General Walter S. Grant; Major General Frank R. McCoy, president of the commission; Major General Blanton Winship; Brigadier General Guy V. Henry; and Brigadier General John T. Kennedy. *Library of Congress.*

years. Due to his prior knowledge of the plot, Anthony Cramer was charged with treason and sentenced to forty-five years in prison, but he appealed his conviction. Cramer pleaded guilty to the lesser charge of trading with the enemy and was sentenced to six years. Harry and Emma Jaques were not tried but held in enemy detention until their deportation to Germany.

After the prosecution, led by Attorney General Frances Biddle, made its case, the eight saboteurs were found guilty and sentenced to death. Six of the eight saboteurs, Herbert Haupt, Edward Kerling, Richard Quirin, Heinrich Heinck, Hermann Neubauer and Werner Thiel, were executed by electric chair on August 8, 1942, and buried in Blue Plains potter's field in Washington, D.C. President Roosevelt commuted Dasch's and Burger's death sentences to thirty years to life in prison because they cooperated with the prosecution.

Luckily, Operation Pastorius failed due to the team members' flawed planning and incompetence. However, the German American Bund collaborators' network was a wake-up call to the internal threat within our country. Our enemies were not only from abroad but were also our citizens, who traded their loyalty and the core ideals of our country for a failed ideology they knew little to nothing about. Ordinary people who never caused any concern with the authorities were recruited through a steady stream of Nazi-funded propaganda. Demagogue-like political leaders, using this propaganda, racial indifference and conspiracies that targeted people's trust in our democratic institutions, rallied thousands to pledge loyalty to Hitler. These rallies of sedition were not conducted in the shadows but in the open, while Bund leaders argued that the United States' democratic principle of free speech allowed them to hold such rallies. New York City and the rural corridor of Long Island may have no resemblance to the Rhine or Bavaria, but they were just as susceptible to turning Nazi. Anti-Nazi activist and journalist Dorothy Thompson once wrote,

> *Kind, good, happy, gentlemanly, secure people never go Nazi….But the frustrated and humiliated intellectual, the rich and scared speculator, the spoiled son, the labor tyrant, the fellow who has achieved success by smelling out the wind of success—they would all go Nazi in a crisis…. Those who haven't anything in them to tell them what they like and what they don't—whether it is breeding, or happiness, or wisdom, or a code, however old-fashioned or however modern, go Nazi.*[8]

The process of finding potential followers of Nazi doctrine who would be willing to destroy their own country or believe Democracy was dead started not in June 1942 but a decade prior, slowly building on biases, distrust, isolationism and frustration. These sentiments were not reserved for any specific class but were embraced by various members of society, including elected officials and well-to-do bankers and industrialists. Overall, Long Island and all five boroughs of New York City would almost drown in an undertow of Nazism.

CHAPTER 2

BREEDING GROUND FOR AN AMERICAN REICH

Over 3,800 miles from Berlin, Germany, across the Atlantic, the smell of salt, pine and honeysuckle is carried by coastal winds blowing over centuries-old farms recessed into pitch pine and scrub oak forests. In many of these pastoral communities, sixty miles east of New York City, homes are referred to by family name instead of street and number. Dozens of these rural hamlets, named from Algonquian land descriptions, were existing communities before European conquest. Isolated by a lack of development, pre–World War II Long Island was a rural appendage of New York City, bearing no resemblance to the current massive suburban developments, strip malls and complex parkways/expressways. Many communities' commercial hubs depended on underdeveloped nineteenth-century dirt farm roads, which resembled the average pre–World War II rural American main street. The total population of Nassau County in 1930 was 303,053, which would rise to 406,748 by 1940. Suffolk County, the least populated of the two counties, had a population of 161,055 in 1930, which grew to 197,355 by 1940. The most populated hamlets were the coastal village centers of Huntington, Freeport, Bay Shore and Patchogue, as well as the more inland community of Rockville Centre—smaller-scale communities developed in the shadows of the various Gilded Age estates. The owners of these estates, who valued the tranquil landscape and privacy, fought against any expansion of roads that would make the surrounding Long Island communities accessible for travel. The main transportation lines for much of the region were the South and North Shore railroad lines, which connected some central Long Island farming communities. One of these communities was Yaphank, a town overwhelmingly isolated from the politics and people of Greater New York.

Before World War I, middle-class first- and second-generation Germans started establishing communities across Nassau and Suffolk Counties, including the surrounding area of Yaphank. In Western Suffolk, less than an hour from Manhattan, the village of Breslau (present-day Lindenhurst) was built by Charles Schleier as a commuter suburb for German immigrants. Several beer halls opened along the main street of Breslau, competing over who offered the most authentic German experience. But the center of the community's pride was Baloney John's Beer Garden and its German festivals. Attempting to build a better, more self-sufficient Breslau, developers Richard and Andrew Wolpert (who embraced American democratic values) built the suburban development of German Town, twenty minutes east of Breslau and within a mile of the Central Islip Psychiatric Center. The Wolpert family envisioned the community becoming a German metropolis in the fresh air of the open countryside and embracing the American ideal of affordable homeownership. In the aftermath of World War I, America had lost 116,516 people; of that number, Nassau and Suffolk Counties lost 347 men from 108 communities and villages. Fearing that their loyalty to America would be questioned and under pressure from the post office, which had been established in 1922, the Wolpert family begrudgingly changed the town's name to Islip Terrace. The growing German population in this community and the surrounding Western Suffolk towns would face discrimination from locals, fostering a German Nationalist movement blended with sympathetic sentiment toward post–World War I Germany.

Locals in many rural communities of Suffolk County had a long-standing distrust of urban areas and outsiders. This distrust was further heightened by the spread of a new strain of influenza, later named the Spanish flu. This pandemic would kill an estimated 100 million people worldwide, including 675,000 Americans. Most states had a patient zero traced to a local military base. Across Long Island, demobilized soldiers coming home stationed in Camp Upton, Suffolk County (a short distance from Yaphank), created the first hot zone cluster of Spanish flu on Long Island and the New York metro area. By October 1918, Camp Upton had 3,050 flu cases. When it came to new cases, no action was taken to isolate those showing symptoms, and they were allowed to interact with local communities. Before the increasing case numbers across Long Island villages and towns were reported to the proper military authorities, many Camp Upton soldiers headed home to densely populated New York City. People welcomed the soldiers home with overcrowded social gatherings, as these veterans shared tales of how they braved the face of death, all unaware they were about to face an invisible death. An estimated 30,000 New York City residents died as a result of the pandemic. Headlines that shared the horrors of the flu pandemic spurred commentary about returning to an isolationist policy globally. Following the influx of cases, mask mandates in densely populated communities were encouraged or enforced, and schools were closed for weeks to reduce the spread of the flu.

Despite the effects of the Spanish flu pandemic, Suffolk County had a robust economy overall. Long Island's commerce depended on agriculture, shellfish harvesting, boatbuilding, summer resorts designed for wealthy/middle-class city residents and residential urban sprawl. The demand for labor from these industries attracted Italians, Jews, Eastern Europeans and African Americans who fled the South to escape from poverty and the violence of the Ku Klux Klan. Despite trying to seek new opportunities, many of these groups bore witness to a significant increase in Ku Klux Klan membership throughout the Long Island region, including the New York City borough of Queens. Driving the rise in Klan membership were rapid demographic shifts (growing Catholic immigrant communities and declining White Anglo-Saxon Protestant populations), fears of Communism and rapidly changing social values.

Klan membership peaked at an estimated one in seven Long Islanders, and local town and county elections were won by pro-Klan candidates.[9] These candidates utilized a culture war platform that portrayed immigrants and city values as infringing on local traditional norms. The Ku Klux Klan flooded local Long Island communities with false newspapers, such as the *Vigilance*, that sensationalized crimes committed by immigrants and Catholic Church corruption. These periodicals reported that New York Governor Al Smith had conspired to make America a colony of the Roman Catholic Church. Other Klan-based news sources, such as *The Kourier Magazine* (in July 1927), declared that the "Catholic church teaches disloyalty to America, and now is trying to invade America by attempting to re-elect Catholic Governor Alfred Smith to promote the breakdown of America and its values."[10] Klan news became more dominant than legitimate newspaper sources, fueling breakaway factions within both major political parties.[11] On February 12, 1923, as they did every year, communities of color celebrated Abraham Lincoln's birthday; however, this time, the celebrations were cut short due to the crimson-flickering flames of burning crosses.[12] Fueled by the media blitz about a Catholic takeover of New York, the Klan started to utilize more aggressive intimidation tactics. On August 7, 1928, the Klan burned down the Little Flower Catholic orphanage in Wading River, Suffolk County.[13] Local Catholic organizations, such as the Holy Name Society, held large-scale rallies declaring the local Klan's actions cowardly attacks against children. In reaction to the Catholic rallies, local store owners and businesses began to hang signs that read "TWAK" (Trade Only With a Klansman) to demonstrate solidarity with local Klan members and their willingness to hire only White Anglo-Saxons.

Spilling into the patchwork of isolated Long Island communities was the fictional book *Protocols of the Elders of Zion*, which detailed a secret conspiracy of Jewish people plotting to take over the world economically and politically. This anti-Semitic book, popularized by Henry Ford, was published in his *Dearborn Independent* newspaper, and over half a million copies were distributed through his Ford auto dealerships nationwide. Local chapters of the Long Island Klan secured copies from these vast dealership networks and spread them to isolated Long Island communities. Klan members were mandated to read *Protocols of the Elders of Zion* and incorporated ritual parades in front of synagogues to strike fear into their congregations. Jewish business owners, such as Freeport pharmacist Ernest Louis, were kidnapped by the Klan in front of village police, who did not intervene due to their anti-Semitic sentiments.[14] The Klan later released Louis on the condition that he and his family leave Freeport.

Compounding the anti-Semitic conspiracy theories, racial biases, lack of trust in the government and isolationist global views, the stock market crashed on October 24, 1929. Over nine thousand banks failed, and wealth that totaled the cost of World War I was lost in the stock market within a week. Throughout the country, unemployment spiked to 25 percent. These economic effects were dire for everyday people on Long Island. Locals who worked on large estates for America's wealthiest people found themselves unemployed, homeless and wandering from town to town in search of stability. Resort communities that were the pride of South Shore towns lay vacant, exposed to the elements. The western parts of Nassau County and eastern Queens, by Thurston's Creek, became known as Hungry Harbor due to the squatter shacks erected by locals who lost their homes to foreclosure. Residents of New York City flooded onto Nassau and Suffolk farms to seek employment. Dozens of hungry people dug through harvested potato fields to see if any small potatoes had been left behind. Farms owned by families for generations broke down into a barter-based economy. Over a decade, crippling economic effects would be felt as the national economy stubbornly remained stagnant in prewar America.

In the early 1930s, world news outlets flooded local theaters with newsreels of the fall of post–World War I democracies across Europe. Fascist Italy laid the groundwork for a fascist Germany, which quickly devoured its neighbors, Austria and Czechoslovakia. Feeding into the growing fascist movement, *Time* magazine declared Adolf Hitler Man of the Year. American ambassador Joseph Kennedy (father of future president John F. Kennedy), witnessing firsthand a growing fascist movement in England with the rise of Oswald Mosley's British Union of Fascists, declared, "Democracy is finished in England. It may be here [in the United States], too."[15]

The global influence of fascism seeped into many small towns across the United States, including ones on Long Island, which started turning to far-right figures and paramilitary groups to validate their biases and anxieties. Many rural Long Islanders' only source of trusted information about the outside world was daily radio shows. Thousands of locals tuned into Father Charles Coughlin's anti-Semitic, pro-fascist weekly radio show or subscribed to his weekly *Social Justice* magazine. Father Coughlin, who often wrote letters of admiration to Italian dictator Benito Mussolini, would become a link between the growing fascist movement in Europe and small-town America, delivering a daily helping of bigoted rhetoric marketed as trustworthy news. Inspired by his broadcast and periodicals, the paramilitary group the Christian Front was formed to overthrow the United States government and replace it with an anti-Semitic fascist government. Feeding into Coughlin's daily helping of racist propaganda was John Burgman's *Station Debunk*. Burgman advertised his short-wave radio show as patriotic, starting every episode with "The Star-Spangled Banner" and the catchphrase "The Voice of Free America." In an average broadcast, the host would denounce "American politicians as influenced by a secret Jewish elite running the government, with the end goal of sending American farm boys to their deaths for Reds."[16]

Inspired by these broadcasts, groups took root locally, including the Christian Crusaders, the Christian Mobilizers and unofficial chapters of an Italian fascist group, the Order of the Black Shirts. Furthering their mobilization was their shared belief that any organized leader or militia could conduct an uprising similar to Hitler's 1923 Munich Beer Hall Putsch. Speakers from these groups fundraised money for Hitler's war machine, recruited people for Nazi espionage networks and attempted to rationalize Nazi ideals as Americanism. Camp Siegfried in Yaphank, Suffolk County, operated ten miles from the region's most extensive military base and thirty miles east of America's most prominent aviation defense plants. German Bund camps like Camp Siegfried were established not just in Yaphank, Long

Island, but also in the communities of New York and the Midwest. These camps interconnected national networks of Nazi training, equipped with a centralized publishing company to promote American Nazism to anyone who would listen. Working in sync with the Bund and Camp Siegfried were Nazi-sympathizing political officials. Elected representatives from both major political parties, who were indifferent, attended rallies as guests of honor. These fascist enablers almost allowed Nazi groups and their demagogues to goose-step us out of democracy by advocating a cure for the failures of democracy by overlooking the evils of fascism.[17]

CHAPTER 3

MYTH BUILDING

The Foundation of the German American Bund

Prince Siegfried lived by the Rhine River in medieval Germany and oversaw his father's Germanic kingdom. The king sent his son, Prince Siegfried, out into the far reaches of his kingdom to prove his worth to the throne with the parting advice, "He who yearns to win fame must not shun toil." Siegfried expanded his family's fortune and kingdom during his adventure to prove himself by tracking down a dragon that oversaw a gold hoard. Siegfried slew the dragon and bathed in its blood, which gave him superhuman powers. With the power bestowed on him by the true treasure, the dragon's blood, he created a golden age for the German Empire by expanding its territory from central to eastern Europe. The tale of Siegfried was rediscovered by Richard Wagner and made into an opera in 1876. In the nineteenth and twentieth centuries, the fable of Siegfried, in opera or fairy tale form, became the centerpiece of the German nationalist movement. Siegfried also became the name of the German American Bund camp in Yaphank, Long Island. Just as the myth of Siegfried was used to fuel German nationalism and, later, the cult of Nazism, the founder of the Bund, Fritz Kuhn, constructed a fable to validate himself as a qualified candidate for führer of a Nazi-friendly America.

Kuhn was born on May 15, 1896, in Munich, Germany. When he was eighteen, Germany entered World War I, and he enlisted in a Bavarian infantry unit. He experienced significant battles, was promoted to lieutenant and was awarded the Iron Cross First Class toward the end of his service. Like many returning soldiers who had experienced the war's defeat, he was cynical about the new republic. Facing the grips of a bad economy and rapid societal changes, Kuhn and many other discharged soldiers embraced the anti-Semitic conspiracies touted in seedy beer halls to explain the state of affairs in Germany. Driven by the disgruntled sentiments of the veterans, paramilitary groups started to take shape, utilizing violence against the politically left-wing ideological movements. Adolf Hitler became the voice of this growing paramilitary movement and one of the founders of the nationalist/fascist group Braunhemden (Brownshirts). As the Braunhemden took root among the emerging right-wing factions across Germany's beer halls, the paramilitary group Freikorps, steeped in Hitler's ideology, grew in numbers. According to Kuhn, he joined the group and, later, Hitler's unified Nazi Party. During Kuhn's membership, he claimed, he participated in the 1923 Munich Beer Hall Putsch, a failed coup to overthrow the local Bavarian government.[18] Nothing in the FBI's records and investigations into Kuhn supports his claim that he participated in the putsch. In the aftermath of the putsch, Kuhn enrolled in the University of Munich and studied chemistry; while attending, he engaged in various acts of larceny.

Attempting to get a fresh start, Kuhn migrated to Mexico and entered the United States via the southern border. He found a job working for Ford Motor Co. in Michigan and saved enough money to relocate to New York, where he absorbed himself in the expanding German Nationalist movement. Amid the various nationalist movements in New York, the pro-Nazi group Friends of New Germany formed a Brooklyn-based chapter in the fall of 1933.

Friends of New Germany was founded in the Detroit area in May 1933 by Heinz Spanknoebel. Spanknoebel was an ordained Seventh-Day Adventist minister in Germany who relocated to Detroit to build a church. He later claimed that his church broke up shortly after he arrived in Detroit, but there are no records of him ever having a church in the United States.[19] While in Detroit, Spanknoebel got a job with Ford Motor Co. He was not known to practice any religion or make any attempt to obtain U.S. citizenship. In 1933, he returned to Germany and met with Nazi Deputy Führer Rudolph Hess about creating a pro-Nazi group in America called Friends of New Germany. It would be a propaganda machine intended to convince German Americans that, as in Germany itself, whatever social and economic ills afflicted America could be blamed on the Jews and the Communists—and that Hitler's vision was the only solution.[20] Law enforcement suspected the organization was a so-called fifth column for the Nazi Reich. Local Friends for New Germany leaders defended the group, justifying it to preserve German culture. In a press statement, a group representative said:

> *We want to maintain our Germanism. German brothers must never be left in the lurch; we must give our brothers abroad the spiritual and moral equipment to fight systematic propaganda lies against the Reich.*[21]

As the Friends of New Germany gained a foothold, Nazi Germany consolidated its 4,700 newspapers, whose total circulation was twenty-five to thirty million. Joseph Goebbels, propaganda minister, would build a savior-like narrative around Hitler and his Nazi followers. The crafted narrative defined the villains, heroes and martyrs of the Nazis' rise to power. Heroes who combated villains like communists and Jewish people were exported to various Nazi-friendly groups worldwide, cementing the narrative across borders. In January 1930, Horst Wessel, a Nazi stormtrooper who got into a fight with two people affiliated with Germany's Communist Party, was shot to death. Albrecht Höhler confessed and was sentenced to six years but died in jail. Wessel was lifted to martyr status within the Nazi propaganda machine through a song composed by Goebbels, "Horst-Wessel-Lied." The song was sung in German during Nazi parades and Friends of New Germany rallies throughout Brooklyn. The lyrics, translated into English, were:

> *The flag is high; our ranks are closed.*
> *The S.A. marches with silent, solid steps.*
> *Comrades shot by the Red Front and reactionaries*
> *March in spirit with us in our ranks.*
> *The street is free for the brown battalions.*
> *The street is free for the stormtroopers.*
> *Millions full of hope, look at our swastika.*
> *The day breaks for freedom and for bread.*
> *For the last time, the call will now be sounded.*
> *For the struggle now, we all stand ready.*
> *Soon will fly Hitler's banners over every street*
> *Our slavery will last only a short time longer.*
> *The flag is high; our ranks are closed.*
> *The S.A. marches with silent, solid steps.*
> *Comrades shot by the Red Front and reactionaries*
> *March in spirit with us in our ranks.*[22]

ORTSGRUPPEN
des
GAUES OST

BROOKLYN, N. Y. (Sitz der Gauleitung)

NEW YORK, N. Y.
BRONX, N. Y.
ASTORIA, L. I.
YONKERS, N. Y.
WHITE PLAINS, N. Y.
POUGHKEEPSIE, N. Y.
BUFFALO, N. Y.
STATEN ISLAND, N. Y.
BAY RIDGE, N. Y.
ROCHESTER, N. Y.
NASSAU COUNTY, L. I.
COLLEGE POINT, L. I.
PHILADELPHIA, PA.
PITTSBURGH, PA.
READING, PA.
HUDSON COUNTY, N. J.
PASSAIC COUNTY, N. J.
NEWARK, N. J.
WASHINGTON, D. C.
BALTIMORE, MD.

Left: The Friends of New Germany circulated an annual yearbook highlighting events and supporters, including this listing of all Friends of New Germany chapters. This would be the groundwork for the later German Bund. *Longwood Library, Bayles Local History Room and Photograph Archives.*

Below: "Horst-Wessel-Lied" became the anthem for the Nazi Party in Germany and later was adopted as the anthem for Friends of New Germany rallies. *University of Wisconsin–Madison Special Collections Postcards.*

In addition to the Nazi anthem, Goebbels created a full-length movie immortalizing Wessel, which the Brooklyn-based Friends of New Germany screened. Friends of New Germany also distributed the film to multiple German American theaters across the tristate area. Some theaters, such as New Jersey's Patterson Theater, banned the movie, stating, "Discord might be created among elements favoring and those objecting to the Nazi regime."[23] The myth of Horst Wessel's martyrdom grew, and the Nazi regime conducted show trials of additional people for the murder almost five years later. Those targeted were anyone who lived in the same building as Wessel and was Jewish or a communist. Two of the additional men tried were nowhere near Wessel's apartment at the time of the shooting, but both were sentenced to be beheaded.

Within months of its creation, the Friends of New Germany took control of the smaller, five-hundred-member German Nationalist group, the Free Society of Teutonia. The German Labor Front, another local pro-Nazi group that fashioned itself from Nazi Labor Minister Robert Ley's policies, had its leadership taken over by Spanknoebel. Other non-Nazi German organizations, such as the United German Society and the Federation of German Jewish Society, openly denounced the Friends of New Germany and Spanknoebel as anti-Semitic Nazi agents. In response to the accusations, Nazi agents threatened dissenting German groups and leaders with denunciation to the authorities in Germany and labeled them saboteurs.[24]

To expand Nazi influence, Spanknoebel focused on taking over the largest German-language news source in the United States, the *New Yorker Staats-Zeitung Und Herold*. In early July 1933, Spanknoebel and a colleague stormed into editor Victor Ridder's office with letters from Nazi Labor Minister Robert Ley and Foreign Division Chief Ernest Bohle, claiming authority to assume control over the paper.[25] Spanknoebel explained to Ridder, "You will no longer be allowed to publish your pro-Jewish articles in this paper." In response, Ridder told Spanknoebel, "Get out and stay out; Berlin's authority does not extend to New York City." Over in Berlin, the *Staats-Zeitung* was widely circulated, but Heinrich Himmler banned the New York–based paper by decree in collaboration with Joseph Goebbels.[26]

Known poet and writer George Sylvester Viereck, who graduated from the College of New York City, built a reputation for his pro-German and Nazi stance. His writings gained the interest of Hitler, who met with him in 1934. After his return to the United States, he became editor of the German Library of Information in New York City and an advisor to German

Ambassador Hans Dieckhoff on issues related to U.S. public opinion. Viereck, a frequent speaker at most Friends of New Germany rallies, would become the speechwriter for chapter leaders who were struggling to engage their base.

The Friends of New Germany's publicized presence and membership attracted a growing local resistance. Daily editorials in the *Brooklyn Daily Eagle* denounced the group's double standard regarding constitutional rights, such as one that read:

> *What are the Friends of New Germany? Americans or Germans? How long would Adolf Hitler tolerate an organization in Germany advocating American principles, wearing uniforms and insignias representing this country? An American, be he naturalized or a citizen by birth, should believe in and uphold the basic principles of our Constitution. That person cannot at the same time be a follower of an opposite principle.*
>
> *Those so-called Americans and Friends of New Germany should go where they can reap all the benefits dealt out by this tyrannical government.*[27]

Groups such as Jewish War Veterans and the newly formed Anti-Nazi Boycott Committee filed numerous legal challenges against the Friends of New Germany, using the state statute that made it illegal to desecrate the American flag. These legal challenges were based on New Germany's failure to display the American flag at meetings.

In the fall of 1933, U.S. Congressman Samuel Dickstein of New York initiated the proceedings to start a congressional investigation into Nazi activities in the United States. Following the announcement of the congressional inquiry, government attorney George Z. Medalie and federal agents issued a warrant for the arrest of Heinz Spanknoebel. The warrant was issued "under the Wartime Act, which provides five years in jail or a $5,000 fine, or both, for 'acting as a foreign governmental agent without notice to the Secretary of State.'"[28] Before agents could arrest Spanknoebel, he was recalled to Germany and sailed from New York to Nazi headquarters in Hamburg to explain the charges.[29] Spanknoebel would never return to the United States; he stayed in Germany and worked on creating propaganda geared toward various German communities abroad.

During the congressional investigation, multiple letters sent from Nazi consuls to Friends of Germany in New York were discovered. One letter from Hamburg-based Chief of Nazi Propaganda Herr Erdman to Heinz Spanknoebel read:

> *A shipment of pamphlets is being sent to our confidential agent, Mr. O. Simon, aboard the Albert Ballin tomorrow. Convinced that we will succeed in our common efforts to win our country's fellow men in the United States to the ideology of national socialism and create understanding and recognition of the Third Reich among American citizens. I greet you and sign with our motto of battle: Versailles Must Fall.*[30]

The House committee found other letters linking films that were being shipped to New York and shown in movie theaters in German-populated areas to Nazi propagandists. The most disturbing find was instructions for creating networks to distribute the propaganda from New York to the Midwest.

In a public statement to the *Times*, a spokesperson for the Nazi government stated:

> *There is no authorized representative of myself or the German National Socialist Party active in America.... I have given the strictest orders that not even lectures or speeches on National Socialism are to be given in America by members of my party. What good would it do me to waste money on propaganda in America? No doubt, Jews are at the bottom of such reports.*[31]

In addition to this public statement, Adolf Hitler issued a decree ordering "German nationals in the United States to give up all membership in any politically active bodies."[32] Nazi Germany's focus on propaganda in the United States would have to be redesigned and geared toward exacerbating U.S. social divides at every level.

The departure of Spanknoebel left the Friends of New Germany in an internal power struggle. Friends of New Germany modified its membership criteria to include only German American citizens to avoid future charges of members being unregistered foreign agents; this modified requirement stripped membership from three thousand active members, isolating the core base of the organization. From the ashes of Friends of New Germany, the German American Bund formed in Buffalo, New York, with Fritz Kuhn at the helm of its leadership. The brief exposure of the congressional hearings did little to discourage membership in this more aggressive organization. During the National Bund Convention in 1938, leadership focused on expanding the group's presence and membership through Americanization. Bund Order number 21 mandated,

> *The Bund must adopt an American front in appearance. All meetings, drill manuals, Bund Newspapers, the Bund anthem (Horst Wessel Lied), and public affairs must be in English, and all designated Bund Storm Troopers must be trained in public speaking. The Bund greetings "Heil Hitler" and "Heil Deutschland" must be changed to "Free America."*[33]

The Bund's membership guidelines under Order 21 remained pro-German, pro-Nazi and anti-Semitic but promoted a stronger anti-communist stance. Meetings open to the public organized by the Bund were held under the name of the Anti-Communist Federation of America. Additional orders from the convention and the Bund's New York leadership mandated weapons training for all SS and Bund commanders. Bund commander Mike Drey, who rolled out the weapons training, stated:

> *Bund members are to look for a good spot for a rifle range. Members would organize separate shooting clubs among chapters, but they must be secretive. These groups have to look like citizen hunting clubs unrelated to the Bund. In the meantime, members should seek NRA (National Rifle Association) membership to access the ranges.*[34]

The Bund leadership budgeted $3 a year per member for NRA membership dues; additional costs included $14 per new gun and $7.50 per used firearm. As Bund members armed themselves and trained with various firearms, chapter leaders were encouraged to form friendships with local police departments, National Guard divisions, army members and the navy.

Unlike the Friends of New Germany, the Bund created several separate companies affiliated with the organization's overall goals. West Coast German Bund leader Herman Schwinn managed the Western German Travel Center. Schwinn, a resident of Los Angeles, received all financing from the New York Bund, but all transactions for travel to Germany through the travel firm were processed by a New York–based third-party company, Hans Utsch and Company. This trio of companies provided currency conversion, travel papers, letters of credit and tickets to German ocean liners leaving New York and trains within Germany to prospective German travelers. Travel papers were expedited through the bureau with exceptional speed due to the partnership between Hans Utsch and Company and the German consulate in New York. All Bund leaders throughout the country had travel expenses to the Reich paid for by the Nazi government. While Bund members visited Germany to embrace Nazism, some resettled in the

HEIL! HEIL!

All Germans and Aryans of Pure Nordic Blood!

We Have the JEWS on the Run!
Let Us Keep Up the Good Work!

DO NOT ATTEND

Any Theater showing pictures with any of these Jews or Jew Lovers:

Claudette Colbert is married to a Jew; Norma Shearer was married to a Jew; Margaret Sullivan was married to a Jew; Eddie Cantor is a Jew; Al Jolson is a jew; Sylvia Sydney is a Jew; Ruby Keeler is married to a Jew; and Ricardo Cortez is a Jew.

This is only the Beginning to an End:

WATCH ALL FUTURE DEVELOPMENTS

Join any one of our country wide organizations and clubs chartered for the purpose of eliminating the enemy – the JEW from all Industry!

Become a member of this Legion to make this great country of ours safe from the Jew and Russia.

HEADQUARTERS: San Francisco, California
Charter No. 12

The CCC Camps would make good Concentration Camps for the Jews!

The Bund branched from the East Coast to the Midwest to the West Coast. Its large-scale rallies within German enclaves became its main source of recruitment. Pictured is a poster from a San Francisco rally highlighting the group's Nazi ideals. *Northridge University Library, Digital Collection.*

In the aftermath of Heinz Spanknoebel's return to Germany, the Friends of New Germany lacked leadership. Fritz Kuhn assumed the group's leadership and merged it with the new German American Bund. Kuhn is pictured here *(in the front row and at the center, wearing glasses)* at a Bund rally. *FBI archives.*

Reich permanently. German militarism created a demand for skilled military manufacturing, which inspired Nazi Minister of Labor Robert Ley to ask "all former German nationals to return to the fatherland." Manufacturing cities in Germany would pay for the trip, and the Western German Travel Center would help provide the papers for relocation. Some in New York relocated, but most Germans returning to Germany were from Midwestern cities such as Cleveland. As the travel company grew, it advertised itself in a pro-fascist newspaper, the *Christian Free Press*, as the "Gentile Travel Bureau" and open to people outside of the Bund. The Bund's official publishing company was A.V. Publishing. This company was incorporated as a separate entity from the Bund but was managed by Walter Kappe, Bund leader and cofounder of the German Nationalist group Teutonia Society. A subscription to the newspaper *Deutscher Weckruf und Beobachter* cost $1.50 for six months and $3 for an entire year. Advertised in each edition were the youth camps run by the Bund, which prided themselves on scenic landscapes with a daily dose of Nazism.

CHAPTER 4

INSIDE SIEGFRIED

Bund members were encouraged to visit the many Bund summer camps and retreats throughout the United States. The camps included Nordland in Sussex County and Bergwald in Bloomingdale, New Jersey; Camp Hindenburg in Grafton, Wisconsin; Deutschhorst Country Club in Sellersville, Pennsylvania; and Camp Highland in Windham, as well as Camp Siegfried in Yaphank, New York. A specific goal of these camps was to foster the growth of a Nazi youth movement designed around the one in Nazi Germany. Young campers were taught Hitlerism, discipline and militarism to prepare them for the future of the coming American Reich. Fostering the Bund's vision for an American Legion for Hitler was a series of corporations that managed camp operations, which included trips back to Germany. High-ranking Bund leader Ernst Müeller oversaw the Western German Travel Center/Gentile Travel Bureau for East Coast members and the German American Settlement League. Müeller's German American Settlement League managed Camp Siegfried.

Camp Siegfried started as a forty-five-acre purchase from local property owner James Coombs in early 1935. The land sat at the banks of Swezey's Pond, which encompasses the most northern part of Carmen's River, flowing into the Great South Bay along the South Shore of Long Island. Kuhn would describe the vision for Siegfried as: "a little piece of German soil—a Sudetenland in Amerika—planted on this side of the ocean."[35] The tract of land would later be subdivided for seasonal cottages and camp facilities. The roads traversing the camp were named after members of the Nazi high

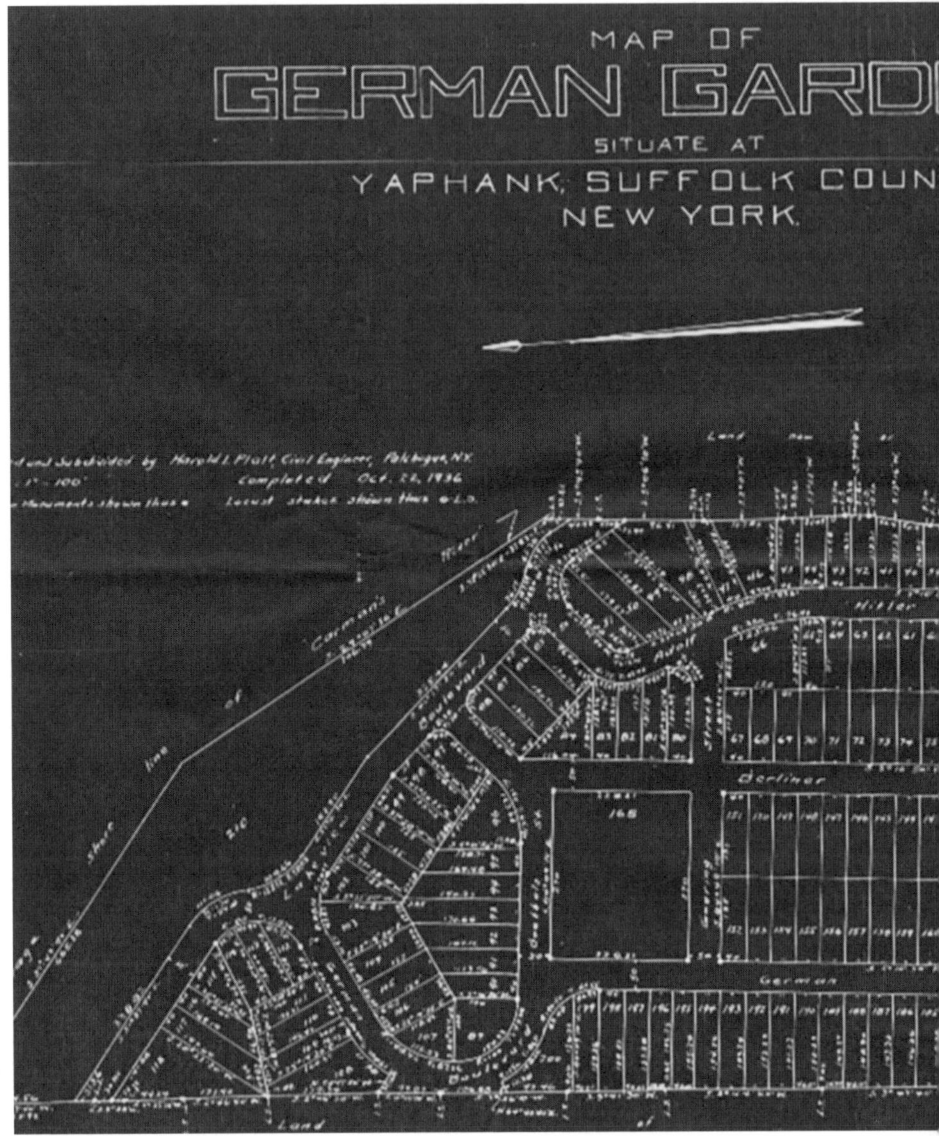

command, such as Adolf Hitler Street, Joseph Goebbels Street and Hermann Göring Street. At the center of Siegfried was the camp's community house, named Hindenburg Platz, which featured hundreds of copies of various Bund/Nazi newspapers and postcards sold in kiosks, showcasing pictures of marching SS men, the camp and the surrounding area. Along the walls of the lobby hung advertisements for anti-Semitic books with titles like *Wake Up Patriotic Americans, You Are Not Enlightened on the Jewish Communistic Menace to*

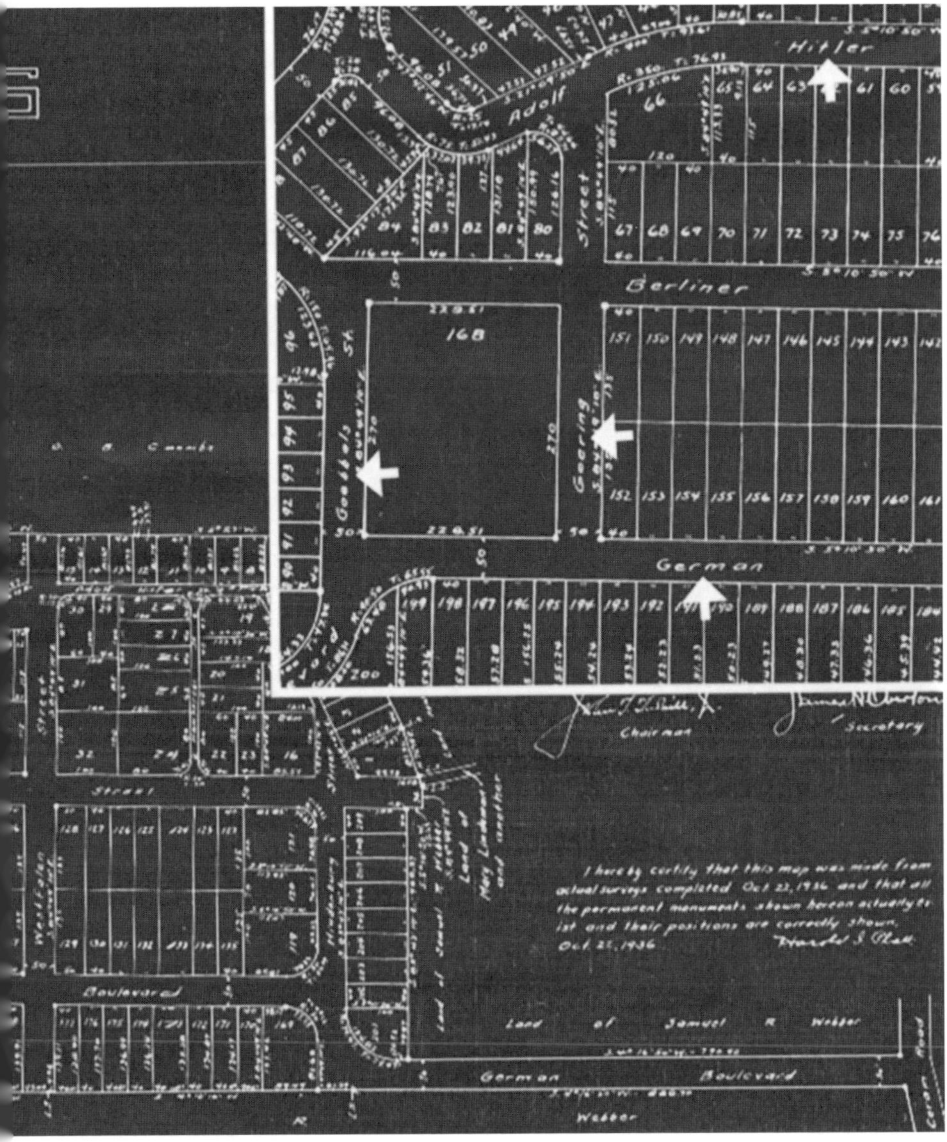

The layout of the planned German American Bund community called German Gardens, 1936. The rezoning of Siegfried would become a fight between the Bund and the Town of Brookhaven. *Longwood Public Library's Thomas R. Bayles Local History Room.*

America, Come and Learn and *A Second World War Is Being Cooked Up for Gentiles to Fight.* Additional Bund and Nazi paraphernalia sold came from a Bund-related wholesale firm, which had a mail-order operation for Bund members not in proximity to a camp. As campers filed into the Hindenburg Platz,

loudspeakers played an ongoing dose of German Nationalistic speeches or prerecorded Nazi speeches made in Germany by the Reich leadership.

Following the grand opening of the summer season, the Long Island Railroad introduced additional train service for visitors to Yaphank, known as the Siegfried Special. This train had a connecting route from Flatbush, Brooklyn, to Yaphank on weekend mornings throughout the summer months. Before the end of the second summer, the camp property was

Left and opposite: Adolf Hitler Street and a tree at the end of the street honoring Adolf Hitler, Camp Siegfried, 1937. *Longwood Public Library's Thomas R. Bayles Local History Room.*

expanded across the lake with the purchase of a large tract of land from a Middle Island resident, Georgia Hammond.

The initial reception from the community was welcoming due to the economic boom from the influx of visitors. Local businesses not related to the Bund that were looking to cash in as merchants for food and supplies displayed signs in their front windows that read "D.K.V." (Deutscher Konsum Verband, which translates to German Consumer Association). The initials signified that the business was against the anti-Nazi boycott and stood in solidarity with the Germans. As the development of the camp expanded, Bund-related companies began to appear along the outer edges of Camp Siegfried. Waldemar Lindemann managed the real estate company German Gardens, which acquired land surrounding the camp and sold it to Bund members seeking a slice of resort-like living. At the entrance to the camp, Bund member Herman Bohlson constructed a beer garden and restaurant known as the Lakeview Inn.

Advertisement for Löwenbräu (Lion's Brew) beer served at the German Day celebration at Camp Siegfried, August 29, 1937. *Longwood Public Library's Thomas R. Bayles Local History Room.*

The entrance to Camp Siegfried. *Longwood Public Library's Thomas R. Bayles Local History Room.*

Camp Siegfried's community square and central flagstaff. *Longwood Public Library's Thomas R. Bayles Local History Room.*

The Camp Siegfried community house. *Longwood Public Library's Thomas R. Bayles Local History Room.*

In the camp, the primary focus was the Bund youth group, later named Junge (Hitler Youth), whose goals were encapsulated in the guidelines of the Bund's charter. The charter affirmed,

> *We want to bring the German youth in the United States, who have, in part, become alienated from the German Fatherland and the German nation, back to the great community of blood and fate of all Germans. To this end, the spiritual regeneration of the Germans after the model of the homeland is necessary. Once attained, there will be strict political schooling.*[36]

While not in camp during the winter, the Junger were mandated to participate in community service and fundraisers. Blue candles sold to Bund members raised money for the travel company Germandom Abroad. The candle symbolized solidarity with Germans abroad as one racial group. During the summer, Siegfried's daily activities for youth members included sports competitions, gymnastics, endurance training, lectures on pro-Nazi philosophies and shooting. Introductory seminars between male youth group members and camp leaders discussed the importance of sacrifice and determination. Camp leaders stated:

> *We want to become men through combat and voluntary sacrifice—that is our determination. As upright men tried through battle and strong in body and soul, we will build the power that no one can destroy. Every one of us is ready to show that it is worthwhile to fight for this holy determination* [Nazism].[37]

This page: Bund members and visitors to Camp Siegfried participating in militaristic exercises inside the Siegfried community house. *Nassau County Photograph Archive.*

Opposite: Camp Siegfried picnic grounds, 1935. *Longwood Public Library's Thomas R. Bayles Local History Room.*

This page: Boys' summer camp tents and Junger (Hitler Youth) campers in 1937. *Longwood Public Library's Thomas R. Bayles Local History Room.*

Militarism was indoctrinated into the youth groups through paramilitary exercises. During the exercises, children were given daggers and told to repeat, "When Jewish blood drips from the knife, then will the German people prosper."[38] If they failed to follow orders, the youth would be assigned to stand at attention for more than an hour or to carry heavy drinking water containers throughout the camp. During all youth events, units of the SS (Schutz Staffel), intended to inspire Bund members, stood guard near all youth activities. The SS guards at the meetings were instructed to develop a rapport with the children, as they were expected to serve as role models and aspire to achieve high-level ranks like their own. The highest rank for the youth to achieve was flag bearer/defender of the Bundesflagge (Bund's Fighting Flag). The daily activities were strictly structured, but Bund leaders ordered camp management not to be too rigid. Leadership feared that if the kids felt too repressed, they might be turned off to Bund/Nazi ideals as they got older. Bund youth were also assigned daily chores around the camp, including clearing brush on newly purchased land.

Every summer brought challenges due to the lack of discipline among preadolescents and adolescents. One of these challenges was a wave of teen pregnancies. A Bund camp attendee, nineteen-year-old Helen Vooros, gave an eyewitness account of Bund leadership and camp activities related to teen pregnancies. She testified in front of the Dies Congressional Committee that Siegfried's counselors told the female campers, "A girl shouldn't be ashamed of having an illegitimate child if the father is German. A girl should produce so that the German population in America should grow, but if a German girl has an association with any other race, that is vile." Vooros elaborated that Theodore Dinkelacker, the Bund Youth Movement leader, told campers, "You should not curb your instincts and go someplace where people can't see you."[39] Many members speculated that the laid-back attitude of camp managers toward the pregnancies was due to the German Nazi Lebensborn program. Lebensborn, started by Heinrich Himmler, encouraged the births of pure German/Aryan children, whether within a marriage or out of wedlock. Under increased pressure from concerned Bund member parents, camp managers assigned chaperones to the younger campers. Tillie Koch, a nineteen-year-old camp volunteer from South Brooklyn, was assigned to monitor and prevent unsupervised nighttime interactions. In August 1937, Tillie developed an upper respiratory infection, and camp managers refused to get her medical attention due to the potential compromised optics of German endurance and strength. Her illness developed into pneumonia, which resulted in her death at the camp. Despite the high teen pregnancy

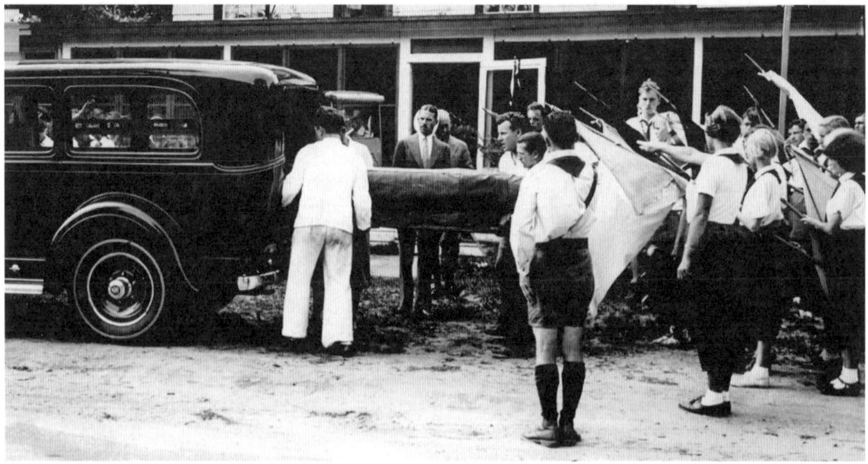

Opposite, top: The Bundee-Kampf-Flagge (Bunds Fighting Flag) at Camp Siegfried's main entrance. The Junger would compete in various military exercises. *Longwood Public Library's Thomas R. Bayles Local History Room.*

Opposite, bottom: Casket of Tillie Koch, who died at Camp Siegfried in August 1937. *Longwood Public Library's Thomas R. Bayles Local History Room.*

This page: In the opening rally at Camp Siegfried, SS and Bund commanders marched in parade formation to the rally stage. *Longwood Public Library's Thomas R. Bayles Local History Room.*

Left: Pastor Heinrich Arent Kropp of St. Paul's German Lutheran Church conducted open prayers and the annual Von Hindenburg religious service. *Longwood Public Library's Thomas R. Bayles Local History Room.*

Below: Camp Siegfried remained insulated from the surrounding community of Yaphank, and trespassers became a concern for the Bund. On the cannon is a reference to Congressman Dickstein, who pushed for congressional investigations into the Bund and its activities. *Longwood Public Library's Thomas R. Bayles Local History Room.*

rates and the death of Tillie Koch, Camp Siegfried had an expansion of new campers the following year.

Increasing attendance at Camp Siegfried led Müeller to consider building permanent housing and attempting to establish a separate city within the Yaphank hamlet. Bund leadership suggested that once the City of Siegfried was established, they would build a chemical factory employing only Bund members on a profit-sharing/cooperative model. This factory would produce a "high-demand chemical" that would be exported (the chemical proposed for production was never disclosed).[40]

CHAPTER 5

RESISTANCE AGAINST THE AMERICAN NAZIS

Within two years of Hitler's Nazi Party taking power in Germany, the Nuremberg Laws (a series of anti-Semitic laws) were enacted. Implemented in 1935, as the Nazis were generating an unprecedented rising tide of anti-Semitic violence, these laws included the Reich Citizenship Law, which declared that only a "pure German" of non-Jewish heritage could be a Reich citizen, and the Protection of the German Blood and German Honor Law, which made it a crime for a pure German to engage in intermarriage or a sexual relationship with a Jewish person. These laws applied to anyone the Nazis defined as Jewish. Any person who had at least three Jewish grandparents (a "full Jew") or who had one or two Jewish grandparents and thus was not pure German (a "mischling" or mixed person) became the target of these laws. Jewish leaders in Berlin, such as the well-known author Rabbi Emil Cohn and Rabbi Dr. Laybaum, were arrested by German police for criticizing the Nuremberg Laws.

New York City and its metro area became the center of Nazi resistance in America. In 1930, the New York metro area was home to an estimated 1.6 million people of Jewish heritage and large Russian, Polish and Eastern European populations who came from areas affected by Nazi laws or military campaigns. Many of these people feared for the safety of loved ones living abroad and closely monitored the breaking news from Europe. However, the most significant collective fear shared by all these groups was the possibility of a Nazi-friendly government establishing itself in their adopted homeland. Fearing for their political survival, many of the elected

Rabbi Stephen S. Wise at a rally in Madison Square Garden. Rabbi Wise was one of the most vocal opponents of the German American Bund. *Library of Congress.*

officials in these communities could not take a neutral stance. In an effort to consolidate collective political power and communicate the growing Nazi threat, various anti-Nazi/anti-fascist groups were developed.

During a state inquiry led by State Senator John McNaboe of New York's Sixteenth District relating to the doctrine the Bund promoted at their summer camps, Fritz Kuhn was asked about the Bund's position on Jewish people. Kuhn responded: "All the Jews are enemies of the United States. Jews are the masterminds behind such communist leaders in this country as Earl Browder" (Browder was an anti-Nazi leader). When members of the inquiry committee protested Kuhn's statement that all Jewish people are communists, Kuhn replied: "If a mosquito is on your arm, you don't stop to ask if it's a good mosquito or a bad mosquito. You just brush it off. We do not consider the Jew as an American. We do not consider the Jew as a man." Senator McNaboe asked Kuhn, "Wouldn't a Jew be an American if he were born here?" Kuhn answered, "Jews are Jews first before they are Americans."[41] After the state inquiry, the headlines across the tristate read, "Kuhn Admits Aims Are Same as Nazis." The public outcry that followed the headlines attracted new members to the multiple anti-Nazi/anti-fascist groups and flooded telegraph/mail rooms with letters to elected officials demanding that they take action against the Bund.

On November 11, 1938, New York District Attorney and future Governor Thomas Dewey declared:

> *The deadly seeds of hate and bigotry have taken a tragic toll in central Europe. They know no boundaries. No one who loves democracy can be content with the misguided notion that the ocean alone will protect us against such poison* [Nazism]. *We must protect ourselves. We must remember the faith in civil liberties and religious liberties of those who founded this country. What happens abroad has a deep and scarring effect on the*

German Bund counterprotest and parade in Yorkville, New York City, near the German Bund headquarters, 1937. *Library of Congress.*

HERRLICH
332
JACOB
HERRLICH
SONS
JEREMIAH T. MAHONEY
ROBERT F. WAGNER, Jr.
VOTE EVERY STAR
MOZART
HALL
FAMOUS
RESTAURANT
BEER WINES

American people. We must not be naïve to the assaults upon democratic rights that cannot pass us by without taking their toll. Any attack on a minority group in any country is an attack on all democracies everywhere.[42]

This statement was a direct response to the Nazi attacks against Jewish people in Germany and rising Nazi paramilitary groups in New York. Dewey's speech was given at a packed New York Anti-Nazi League meeting. Five years before he met with the league, Dewey had various members of the pro-Nazi movement in New York under surveillance. As he moved between jobs in 1934, from an attorney for the United States Southern District of New York to federal prosecutor, Dewey kept himself updated on the Friends of New Germany, the German Bund and any other Nazi activities within the state.

One of Dewey's targets was Colonel Edwin Emerson, president of the Society of American Friends of Germany. From his office in Battery Place, New York City, Emerson had the magazine *Amerika Deutsche Post*, a pro-Nazi and official Friends of New Germany magazine, mass-produced for an anticipated large audience. Emerson's other suspicious activities included daily meetings in the German embassy and trips back and forth to Germany. Dewey's most significant concerns about Emerson were his public influence and credibility as a trusted news source. Emerson was a known newspaper editor and a former member of Theodore Roosevelt's Rough Riders.

Working with Emerson and also being closely monitored was Ralph Easley, director of the anti-Semitic and anti-communist group the National Civic Federation (NCF). NCF, a well-established think tank for Republicans, cowrote and lobbied for labor laws such as the Workmen's Compensation Act and New York child labor laws. NCF's goal was to reduce worker unrest and the influence of communism and preserve American capitalism's ideals. With the rise of Nazism, Easley seized the opportunity to build on anti-communist ideas by importing books from Nazi Germany and translating them into English. One such book was *Communism in Germany*, which Emerson distributed through his magazines and newspaper subscriptions.

Another group working with Emerson in disseminating his Nazi propaganda was the Order of 76. This group's founder was Royal Scott Gulden, who operated the organization as an American patriot group on East Fifty-Third Street, Manhattan. Gulden, who boasted he had one hundred thousand members motivated by true American patriotism, argued:

> *We are defenders of our Republican, or rather Democratic (since Roosevelt became president), form of Government. I have been telling my men that the time will soon come when we shall have to arise to defend this nation against the challenge of Fascist and Communist organizations.*[43]

Despite Gulden's claims of patriotism, he trained his members to watch large groups of Jewish people and suspected communists and document their daily movements. This documentation, along with the successful merger of the Order of 76 with William Dudley Pelley's Nazi group, Silver Legion (Silver Shirts), was to be used in service of the end goal: an "American Pogrom." Once the Silver Shirts and their allies had conducted a purge of Jewish people and a re-enslavement of African Americans, Pelley would fulfill his vision of what he called "Christian Economics." The Pelley economy would redistribute resources confiscated from Jewish people and African Americans to all pure White citizens through a guaranteed income.[44]

The rise of these domestic groups, compounded by events in Germany, caused former New York State Appellate Judge Joseph Proskauer to grow concerned over national security. Within a year, Proskauer collected information about the propagandists and militia groups through his access to informants and various legal proceedings. After leaving the bench in 1930, Proskauer became an active partner in Proskauer, Rose & Paskus, which was contracted to provide legal advice to governmental prosecutors. Once Proskauer consulted with lawyers on the legalities of the intel, the dossier was shared with Congressman Samuel Dickstein, who was on the Committee on Un-American Activities. This intel would be the foundation of the congressional investigation into Nazi propaganda in the United States.

Moving faster than any congressional investigation was the grassroots antifascist movement, which established itself in every borough of New York City and parts of Long Island. As the pro-Nazi groups Friends of New Germany, Order of 76 and the German American Bund evolved, an organized resistance swiftly followed. Groups such as Jewish War Veterans, Friends of Zion, the Anti-Nazi League and various labor unions formed an Anti-Nazi Federation, which took their resistance to the streets within communities that shared Nazi sentiments. In early May 1934, the Anti-Nazi League applied for a permit to protest in front of the Friends of New Germany headquarters in Yorkville. Understanding the potential for violence and the threat to public safety, New York City administrators rejected the permit. Using the rejection of the permit, the league mobilized the Steel and Metal Workers Industrial Union and Workers of Gold Tee Knit Sportswear to send hundreds of telegrams to Mayor Fiorello LaGuardia demanding "the right to parade on the streets of Yorkville against the fascist menace" (the Friends of New Germany and German American Bund).[45] With the rejection of the parade permit and lack of response from the telegrams, additional organizations, including Jewish Workers, People's Committee Against Pogroms and Anti-Semitism, National Students League and International Labor Defense, agreed to join the protest regardless of proper permits. On May 10, the scheduled protest of the Anti-Nazi League evolved into the United Anti-Nazi Conference, which included four additional groups and three thousand protestors. Fifty policemen and ten mounted officers attempted to disperse the crowd as it marched down Second Avenue and Eighty-Fifth Street toward Yorkville. Pro-Nazi onlookers, members of the Bund and Friends of New Germany threw paving stones at the demonstrators and shouted at them to "go home." When the protestors finally dispersed, forty-one anti-Nazi demonstrators were arrested. Later in the evening, the protestors went to Brownsville, Brooklyn, to participate in another organized demonstration to burn thousands of dollars' worth of products made in Germany.

As the summer of 1935 approached, the anti-Nazi protests became more organized and brazen. The German-owned and -operated ocean liner SS *Bremen* was docked at Pier 86 on the West Side of Manhattan, full of German-bound passengers. Before the ship embarked, the Nazi swastika flag was hung on its mast, which attracted anti-Nazi protestors. As demonstrators assembled at the pier holding signs saying, "Nazism Breeds War" and "Nazi Terror," dozens forced their way through security, got on the boat, cut down the Nazi flag and threw it in the Hudson River.[46] This act triggered protestors and crew members to engage in a melee on the ship's deck. Over 150 policemen were dispatched to the boat to break up the fight, resulting in the arrest of nine protestors. In response to the anti-Nazi protest and brawl, the German Steuben Society of New York, in a letter to the city mayor and governor, stated: "Demonstrations that consisted of a howling mob of a thousand or more who threatened violence created a scene which is a disgrace to this city."

The mass protests against German ocean liners and German-made products had limited success, but they marked the first time all these anti-Nazi groups unified. These groups began operating as one with shared guiding ideas and became an effective tool for German economic boycotts. The next focus of this unified resistance was Nazi Germany hosting the 1936 Summer Olympics in Berlin. Hitler and Nazi Germany were going to use the global event to showcase the successes of Nazism in Germany and the superiority

Anti-Nazi protest marching toward Yorkville, New York City. *Northridge University Library, Digital Collection.*

Anti-Nazi League cartoon: "You don't have to sink the ship to drown the rats." The rats represent communism, fascism and Nazism. *New York Public Library Digital Image Collection.*

Members of the American League for Peace and Democracy picketing the Italian embassy. The group protested fascists and Nazis in 1939. *Library of Congress.*

of the so-called pure Aryan. The prior year, the United States had agreed to participate in the games, with Germany's assurance that there would be no discrimination against Jewish athletes. By the summer of 1935, a growing mobilization of religious groups, Jewish leaders and sports clubs had joined with the Anti-Nazi League and labor unions to demand a boycott of the Olympic Games. On August 8, 1935, twenty thousand people—members of the Anti-Nazi League, labor unions, student activists and concerned anti-Nazi individuals—attended a mass meeting in Madison Square Garden to demand that the United States boycott and not attend the games. At the entrance hung a sign that read, "Three dollars for a casket for Adolf Hitler," with a collection jar underneath for donations. On the stage, a giant banner read, "Drive the Nazi terror gangs out of New York City."

The meeting started with the host drawing the audience's attention to six of the nine men arrested for storming the German ship the SS *Bremen*, who had been released from police custody. The crowd in the arena erupted in a standing ovation for the six men. One of the keynote speakers, Morton

Singer, chairman of the Anti-Olympic League, demanded a resolution calling for Germany's "immediate cessation of the barbarous murder and torture of anti-Nazi political prisoners and pogroms against Jews and Catholics."[47] A resolution was proposed and adopted to urge the Amateur Athletic Union not to certify its athletes for participation in the Olympic Games. After the meeting, Catholic priests in attendance wrote an article published in *The Commonweal*, a widely circulated Catholic periodical, stating that due to the breakup of Catholic youth groups and random raids on Catholic cathedrals in Germany, "No Catholic and no friend of the sports activities of a Catholic institution ought to make the trip to Berlin." The article went on to "summon every organization identified with the church to make it clear to its members that participation in the games means an endorsement of willful and violent persecution."[48]

By the fall of 1935, universities had taken up the boycott. Columbia University's student newspaper, *The Spectator*, demanded that the school's board members call on all students or anyone affiliated with the school not to participate in the games. Despite the mobilization of various groups and their shared concerns, the American Olympic Committee refused to take up any form of boycott. Dr. John Brown Jr. of the Olympic Committee, in rebuttal to the protests, stated:

> *There are other ways in which American citizens can express their disapproval of Nazi German discrimination against Jews than by withdrawing from the games. It would be impossible to hold the 1936 Olympics anywhere other than in Berlin, and it would be a great mistake for the American Olympic Committee to withdraw at this time. And we should not allow political, racial, or religious differences to interfere.*[49]

In a last-ditch plea for a boycott, ten thousand anti-Nazi demonstrators marched down Eighth Avenue during peak rush hour, demanding that the United States not participate in the games. The last-minute effort had no impact on the Olympic Committee. In another attempt to wage a protest, the Jewish Labor Committee organized a rival athletic festival called the World Labor Athletic Carnival, held on New York City's Randall's Island on August 15 and 16, coinciding with the Berlin games.[50] Mayor LaGuardia volunteered as one of the chairmen for the carnival's athletic committee, and New York Governor Herbert Lehman was designated to award championship trophies. Five hundred people participated in the games, and spectators' admission fees were donated to various anti-Nazi causes. The overall campaigns to boycott the Berlin games failed. However, they showed the speed and effectiveness of anti-fascist groups in mobilizing around a shared issue, regardless of whether they were anti-communist or communist, religiously affiliated or secular.

The momentum of the anti-Nazi boycott depended on recruiting participants through reading materials such as the Brooklyn-based magazine *Uncle Sam*. Editor Charles Weiss marketed *Uncle Sam* not only as anti-Nazi and anti-fascist but also anti-communist in an attempt to draw a more moderate base of readers. One of the most successful boycotts promoted by the magazine was that of the heavyweight championship match between James Braddock and German boxer Max Schmeling in Madison Square Garden's Long Island City Arena on June 10, 1937. Samuel Untermyer, founder of the Anti-Nazi League, stated the boycott aimed to "deprive Schmeling, a citizen of Nazi Germany, any chance to regain a championship and at the same time preclude the possibility of American dollars finding their way to the Third Reich."[51] Due to the pressure from the boycott, Joe Gould, Braddock's manager, stated he would "not allow Braddock to defend his title if there was nothing in place to prevent the transfer of anything to Germany." The alternative plan Gould proposed was for Braddock to fight Joe Lewis, who had been knocked out by Schmeling the year prior.[52] Despite concerns about American dollars finding their way to the Third Reich, Colonel J. Reed Kilpatrick, president of Madison Square Garden; James J. Johnson, director of the Boxing Commission; and Mike Jacobs, promoter of the boxing match, paid Schmeling a $31,000 advance. In a statement, James Johnson said, "The proposed boycott is absurdly at variance with every American conception of sportsmanship and fair play."[53] The commission's actions and statements had little to no effect on reversing Gould's decision that Braddock would not fight Schmeling. Braddock would fight Joe Lewis instead, in Chicago's Comiskey Park.

In response to all the local, city and international boycotts against Nazi Germany, German propaganda minister Joseph Goebbels warned "Jews outside of Germany that their behavior as well as that of the German Jews would determine future treatment of Jews within the Reich."[54] The success of the Braddock and Schmeling boycott inspired the Bund leadership to try a new tactic. During its 1938 convention, the Bund rolled out the concept of creating holding companies for German-made products or companies managed by Bund members. These holding companies would distance products or services from Nazi and affiliated organizations. During the convention, West Coast leader Herman Schwinn stated,

In the spirit of Minister Göring's Four-Year Plan, the Bund should take over this country's importing business of German goods. It is our duty to break the boycott of German goods, and the holding corporations are going to do something about it. Secondly, a mail-order house is planned to focus on selling German goods in rural areas.[55]

Additional reactions throughout New York City from Bund members and pro-Nazi sympathizers were more aggressive. In the evening hours on April 22, 1938, the headquarters of *Uncle Sam* magazine, located at 130 Flatbush Avenue, Brooklyn, was assaulted by four suspected German American Bund members. Editor Charles Weiss was strong-armed and kicked in the groin and had swastikas carved into his body.[56] After beating and disfiguring Weiss, the four men ripped down an American flag and shredded it into pieces. The following day, the Anti-Nazi League started the paperwork to get its members pistol permits. J.H. Steel, executive secretary of the league, stated:

The police took no action against the Bund and had the attitude of not bothering them because America believes in freedom of speech. Yet one of the pillars of the Nazi program consists of the destruction of free speech. If we who believe that Nazidom is the greatest threat in America today are forced to fight to protect the freedom of our expression, we're willing to do it.[57]

Grassroots anti-Nazi groups were not the only threat to the Bund; investigative journalism exposed the threats posed by the Bund and its followers. The *Chicago Sunday Times* noticed an increase in the Bund's presence throughout the Midwest. Reporter John C. Metcalfe went undercover within the Bund using the name Hellmut Oberwinder. After joining the Bund, Metcalfe documented every activity and conversation he could and published them in his column "I Am a U.S. Nazi Storm Trooper." Metcalfe was sent to New York and attended multiple events at Camp Siegfried as a guest. His observations of the Siegfried rallies were published in his first column:

The regimented tread of marching men under the flaming Nazi swastika resounds from coast to coast in the United States today. In uniforms strangely suggestive of those worn by Adolf Hitler's Nazi storm troops, a relatively small but rapidly growing army is preparing for the American counterpart of "Der Tag" (The Day) when it plans to seize control of the United States. "We are not plotting a revolution," leaders tell their followers. "But

> *we are going to be prepared to wrest control from the communist Jews when they start their revolution. We will save America for white Americans."*[58]

After befriending senior Bund member Alfons Brem, Metcalfe was sponsored for membership by Brem and paid the $1.25 application fee, $0.75 for his first month's membership and an additional $0.50 donation. Metcalfe recalled that during the first meeting he attended as a member, Long Island chapter leaders stated:

> *Democracy has not helped the poor people of this country. The Jews represent five percent of the population, and they are in complete control of the government, Wall Street, and entertainment. Look at the men around Roosevelt in Washington. All Jews are running the country like a dictatorship.*[59]

Within a few months, Metcalfe joined the SS ranks of the Bund. This rank had members undergo weapons training. On his first training day, Metcalfe explained: "Everyone knows that someday bullets will fly in America. When that day comes, we want to be prepared to fight for National Socialism." Metcalfe's reports of anti-Semitic conspiracy preaching, tied together with paramilitary training, spurred awareness of the potential dangers of American Hitlerism. However, Metcalfe made his most significant contribution as a key witness in the House Un-American Activities Committee (Dies Committee) investigations into the Bund and its threat to the United States.

Metcalfe's notes and firsthand accounts revealed extensive yet questionable mailing lists. James Wheeler-Hill, the Bund secretary in the national office in Yorkville, mailed members and other pro-fascist individuals forty thousand copies of Bund speeches. His mailing list was the center of the Dies congressional investigation. Metcalfe stated that the Bund's mailing lists and the propaganda the Bund sent came from "'Letterhead' organizations with no members but were well funded. Evidence shows that these Letterhead outfits come from Germany and potentially from German Ambassadors."[60] During the Dies hearing, when asked how the Bund got its extensive mailing lists and what ties the group had to the Nazi government, Fritz Kuhn stated,

> *I denounce as unqualifiedly false statements of John Metcalfe. The Bund's only ties with Germany are those of sympathy for its emancipation from the oppressions of the Treaty of Versailles.*[61]

Journalist John Metcalfe demonstrates how he went undercover in the Bund as Hellmut Oberwinder. *Library of Congress.*

The eyewitness accounts presented at the Dies congressional hearing into the Bund would build on additional investigations against Nazi sympathizers and their enablers who were connected to high-ranking United States governmental officials.

As the resistance against the Bund intensified in New York City and in the national headlines, a new battlefront in rural Long Island started to take shape. In Yaphank, Camp Siegfried wore out its welcome among most locals. As the Nazis expanded their territory in Europe, news of their atrocities made headlines. Locals who viewed Siegfried as a harmless summer camp became concerned about the paramilitary exercises. Gustave Neuss, who served on the Brookhaven town board from 1933 to 1937 (Yaphank is within the town of Brookhaven), took on the Bund as a centerpiece of his administration. Neuss's first action was documenting who was coming in and out of Siegfried. He recruited Yaphank's Young People's Club members to walk around Siegfried's parking lot and copy down all the license plate numbers.[62] After compiling the plate numbers, he sent a copy to the local New York offices of the FBI. Neuss's additional actions restricted the spread of the Bund facilities within Yaphank. He rejected any construction or zoning permits for the camp until a survey was completed and approved by the town. The original land zoning was B classification, restricting the construction of multiple subdivisions and light commercial developments. Zoning approval was essential to generate revenue for the Bund through sales of summer cottages and year-round housing, as per its new vision for a planned community. In a press release, Ernst Müeller, head of the German-American Settlement League, fed into the racial biases of greater Long Island, stating,

> *The town board has to stop picking on us. If they want a fight, they can have it. We will sell the property to the lowest bidder—a Negro group. How would you like to have Father Divine* [a well-known African American minister] *here? This will ruin the sales and values of the surrounding area.*[63]

Müeller explained that the Bund would move the camp north to Shoreham after the sale. Despite Neuss's determination to reject the permits, planning board members compromised by granting the Bund class C and D zoning. This would allow the Bund to build the number of houses it wanted and provide the subdivision of seventy-five-by-one-hundred-foot lots.

In response to Neuss's tactics against the camp, Fritz Kuhn declared, "German-Americans will have Judge Neuss defeated in his reelection bid." Local leaders of the Bund ordered its members to register as voters in Yaphank to vote out Neuss. In his reelection speech, Neuss addressed the Bund voting drive:

> *They are going to punish me for daring to criticize an organization that I insist has no right to exist in our United States. Every veteran should be insulted to listen to the* Bund *people talk about their Americanism.*[64]

As the 1937 campaign between Neuss and his party's Republican challenger heated up, local veterans turned to acts of vandalism toward the camp. Locals ripped up the swastika flower bed and painted "Down with Hitler" on a nearby wall.

The fall 1937 campaign resulted in a political defeat for Neuss. However, the attention Siegfried and its leaders received from their public fight with Neuss attracted outraged members of the Disabled War Veterans of America to mobilize for a fight. Roy Monahan, leader of the Disabled

American Veterans of the World War, New York state branch, sent member and reporter Syd Boehm of the *New York Journal-American* undercover in Camp Siegfried to inquire about joining the German American Settlement League. Boehm's visit contrasted with Metcalfe's work in that it focused on the local German American Settlement League. While undercover, Boehm tried to join the league and rent a cottage at the camp. He discovered that he must join the German American Bund before joining the league, which required taking an oath.[65] However, according to the New York Civil Rights Law (known as the Walker Law), any organization that requires an oath must file a list of its members with the New York secretary of state. New York State enacted this law in 1920 to combat the influence of the Ku Klux Klan.

After the violation was documented, Monahan filed an official complaint against the league. In May 1938, at a Bay Shore courthouse fifteen miles west of Siegfried, six of the camp managers, Ernst Müeller, Henry Wolfgang, Bruno Haernel, Herman Schwarman, Addo Bielefeld and Henry Hauck, were arraigned in front of Judge Moses W. Drake. The district attorney, Lindsay Henry, argued that the defendants sent multiple letters threatening Monahan and the court officers. In a rebuttal, defense attorney Herman J. Schoenfeld stated: "Did any of these defendants threaten you?" District Attorney Henry replied, "The Volks Bund signed the letters."[66] At the close of the opening arguments, Judge Drake ordered the defendants to be held on $1,000 bail. All seven indictments were related to violating the New York Civil Rights Law, which came with a fine of $1,000 and a year in jail per defendant and an additional $10,000 fine levied against the German American Settlement League. Representing the six, Schoenfeld asked for a bail reduction and was denied. For the next court date, the Bund retained James Murray, who promptly organized a legal team to discredit the district attorney's argument that the Bund imposed a mandated oath. The judge scheduled the trial for July 6.

While awaiting trial, the Bund attempted to hold rallies and their annual carnivals in the village of Lindenhurst. The main topic at these events was the upcoming trial of the Siegfried Six and fundraising to pay for their legal counsel. However, the Bund's rallies drew smaller crowd sizes due to the media attention and growing resistance from the American Disabled Veterans. Additional pushback came from the American Legion and the Knights of Columbus, who successfully petitioned the Lindenhurst village board to create a flag ordinance that banned the display of the American Bund Flag and postponed any permits for Bund events pending review.

Anti-Nazi flyer produced by the Disabled Veterans of America. *United States Holocaust Museum.*

In an appeal, Wilheim Kunze, director of the regional Bund chapters, demanded a reversal of the ban on displaying the Bund flag and to be granted permits for future events. The board upheld the ban and revoked the Bund's licenses for all events, including its annual Pfingstfest festival (German Day Celebration).

During his investigation of the camp and before the trial, Roy Monahan wrote to Lindenhurst Police Chief Edward Morlock, sharing information he'd discovered about the buildup of a violent paramilitary force that could endanger the residents of the village. In reaction to the potential danger, Suffolk County District Attorney Fred Munder went to Washington to confer with Congressman Samuel Dickstein about a congressional investigation into the Bund's activities. In a statement, Dickstein warned:

> *My attention has been called to an application by the Bund in your fair city. If such a parade occurs, Americans will resent and resist the procession of goose-stepping uniformed parades along city highways, resulting in serious complications. Given past experience, the community and the public should be protected by denying an application for such a goose-stepping parade.*[67]

To defuse the American Legion's resistance, Bund leadership invited local American Legion and state legion commander Jeremiah Cross to Camp Siegfried's Fourth of July celebration. In a public reply, Cross said, "If the American Legion ever goes to Camp Siegfried, it will go deputized and on business, not as a guest." During the Fourth of July celebration, four thousand American Legion members and Cross himself did show up at the gates of Camp Siegfried to protest its Fourth of July celebration and denounce the Bund as un-American. Their large presence and the fear of potential violence required law enforcement to protect the Bund members coming in and out of the camp from the American Legion.

On July 6, the trial's opening day, Henry called witness Willy Brandt to the stand. Brandt was a trained Bund stormtrooper who attended all the summer events at Siegfried. When Brandt was asked if he'd witnessed any loyalty oaths to the Bund, he replied, "Yes, it is given to all new members in German." When asked about the English translation of the oath, Brandt stated,

> *In English, it is translated as: "I pledge faith to my leader, Adolf Hitler. I promise Adolf Hitler and those put in charge by him and well known to me or by means of the insignia to be recognized as superiors, loyalty, and obedience, and oblige myself to execute all commands carefully and without personal regard because I know that my leader does not ask anything unlawful of me."*[68]

When asked about how the Bund oath could conflict with the process of obtaining U.S. citizenship, Brandt testified that camp manager Henry Hauck told him:

> *If you tell the judge that you would fight for the United States in the case of a war with Germany, you would be lying as a Nazi. If you say you would fight for the Nazis, you wouldn't get your citizenship papers. The thing to do is just say you will do your duty as a citizen and let the judge figure it out for himself.*[69]

The next witness Henry called to the stand was German Bund member Martin Wunderlich. Henry asked Wunderlich to demonstrate the standard Nazi salute given at Siegfried. Wunderlich showed the court the salute, and Henry asked: "Is that the American salute?" Wunderlich replied, "No, but it will be."[70] In a rebuttal to Brandt's and Wunderlich's testimony, the defense lawyer claimed the oath was not mandatory for German American Settlement League members.

The last witness Henry called was *New York Journal-American* reporter Robert Levitt. On the stand, Levitt described meeting with Müeller to share his thoughts about Roy Monahan. Müeller told Levitt: "We'll take care of him [Monahan] if it takes every cent we've got, and we've got over $100,000. Some dark night, we'll take care of him."[71] Lawyers for the defendants rejected the idea that Müeller threatened Monahan and argued that the statement was taken out of context. However, the defense's arguments did not convince the jury. After fifteen minutes of deliberation, the jury returned with a guilty verdict on all seven counts of violating the New York Civil Rights Law. Judge Barron Hill sentenced Ernst Müeller to a year in jail and a $500 fine, which resulted in Müeller being taken into custody by the Suffolk County Department of Corrections. The other five defendants, Henry Wolfgang, Bruno Haernel, Herman Schwarman, Addo Bielefeld and Henry Hauck, were sentenced to a one-year suspended sentence, each ordered to pay a $500 fine. In closing, Judge Hill ordered the German American Settlement League to pay a $10,000 fine.

As a result of the fines and convictions, the New York State Alcohol Beverage Control Board revoked Camp Siegfried's beer and liquor license. During one of the first rallies at Siegfried after the convictions, on July 17, two thousand Bund members attended. This rally was estimated to be less than one-third the size of the pretrial rallies. As Bund members gathered in the center of the camp for the Jamaica Bund unit's annual flag-raising, a low-flying plane dropped over twenty-five thousand leaflets promoting Americanism into the crowd. The Non-Sectarian Anti-Nazi League had chartered the plane. The blue and white flyers read, "This is a real American." They detailed how tolerance, social equality and loyalty define true American values. Other flyers listed the advantages of living in a country governed by the people, not dictators.[72] In a statement to the local press, members called the incident a violent act due to a bundle of flyers that almost fell on three people, which could have caused injury.[73]

In an attempt to close Siegfried and collect the $10,000 fine, Suffolk County Sheriff Jacob Dreyer started foreclosure proceedings to satisfy the fine by forcing a sale of the property. In response, Fritz Kuhn stated that "the league would not pay the fine, and the county would not be able to padlock the property because all the buildings did not belong to the league but to individuals."[74] The following day, Kuhn announced he would file an appeal on behalf of all six defendants and the camp in the state supreme court. Müeller was released from the Suffolk County jail two weeks after his arrest, pending appeal. By November, the state appellate court in Brooklyn had

Members of the German Bund on trial in Bay Shore. *Courtesy of the Nassau County Photograph Archive.*

reversed the convictions of all six men and the judgment on Siegfried. The justices ruled that there was not sufficient evidence for the initial indictments. In a press release, Kuhn stated,

> *As a result of the court's reversal, several new Bund camps will be established in the surrounding area of Yaphank* [believed to be in Wading River]. *These new camps will be developed on a 300-acre tract of land closer to the Long Island Sound with a mix of summer and residential communities.*[75]

Following the court proceedings, the Bund attempted to hold multiple rallies to build on its members' image as American patriots and to argue that their right to free speech was being violated. Camp Siegfried's annual mid-August rally attracted an estimated forty thousand people in a show of solidarity.

In November 1938, the Nassau County Bund petitioned to rent the auditorium at Nassau County Police Headquarters in Mineola. The following week, the anti-fascist group American League for Peace and Democracy, the labor union CIO and members of the congregations of the Sons of Israel of Woodmere and Temple Beth El of Cedarhurst organized demonstrations in front of the police headquarters, demanding that the Bund be barred from having its rally. To appease the growing protest, the Nassau County Police Department spokesperson, Frank McCahill, announced, "No stormtrooper uniforms are allowed at the rally." In response to criticism for not restricting the meeting, McCahill said,

> *The constitution and precedent prevent us from doing anything other than permitting this meeting, whether objected to or not by some classes of people. As long as the meeting is maintained lawfully and in an orderly manner, we have no interest in it.*[76]

Despite McCahill's attempt to appease the protesters, the crowd increased in front of the headquarters. To give the crowd a voice, Police Commissioner Abram Skidmore invited the leaders of the protesting organizations to discuss the permit process for the Bund. After the leaders conferred with the commissioner on the un-American activities of the Bund, the Bund's request to rent the auditorium was rejected. The Bund announced two days before the scheduled rally that it would move its event to Tulip Hill Hall at 413 Tulip Avenue, Floral Park, a few miles from the police headquarters in Mineola. The last-minute announcement provided little to no time for protesters to demand that the Bund's permit be revoked. The speakers at the rally included Bund leader George Kunze, who asked, "Are the attacks against the German American Bund justified?"; friend of the Bund Sued Maufarrig, speaking on the "Arab Side of the Palestine Question"; and keynote speaker Fritz Kuhn, who closed out the rally. But this rally and the resistance to it were dwarfed by the Washington's birthday rally on February 20, 1939, in Madison Square Garden.

CHAPTER 6

BATTLE FOR MADISON SQUARE GARDEN

On January 29, 1939, the first advertisements for the "Washington's Birthday and Americanism" rally were posted around Manhattan's Yorkville section. The rally, sponsored by the Bund, argued for the organization's definition of true Americanism. A flyer stated:

> *The rally is a defense of the flag, constitution, and Nationalism of the United States and the right to proportionate representation in the conduct of the Nation of the more than a hundred million Aryan (White Gentile) Americans as the only means of preserving our country's Independence and sovereignty and Christian Culture and Civilization.*

Bund mailings advertising the rally to members and allies of Nazism took a defensive tone:

> *The malicious and poisonous attempts to silence and cripple us* [Bund] *by lying press and radio propaganda, by attempted riots and coercion of hall owners to block meetings and fraudulent indictments and convictions (consider the so-called Camp Siegfried Case of Riverhead which has ended in a reversal of the decision by the higher court and complete exoneration of all the defendants) prove that the subversive Jewish-Marxist powers are directing mortal fear of our American Citizenry.*

All who received flyers could preorder tickets for $1.10 in the orchestra pit or $0.40 in the back row.

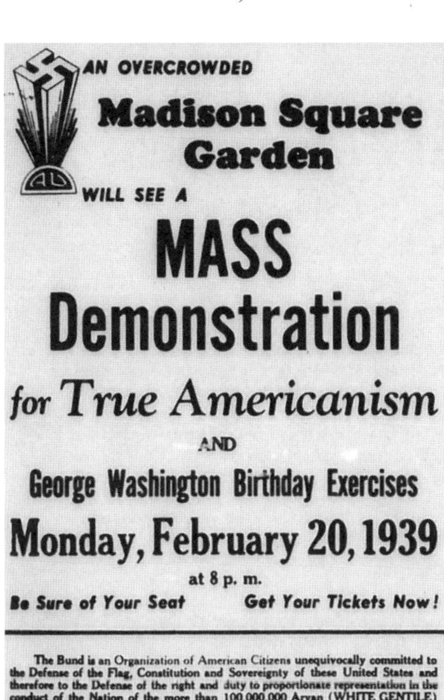

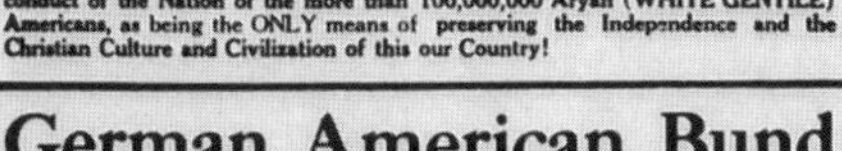

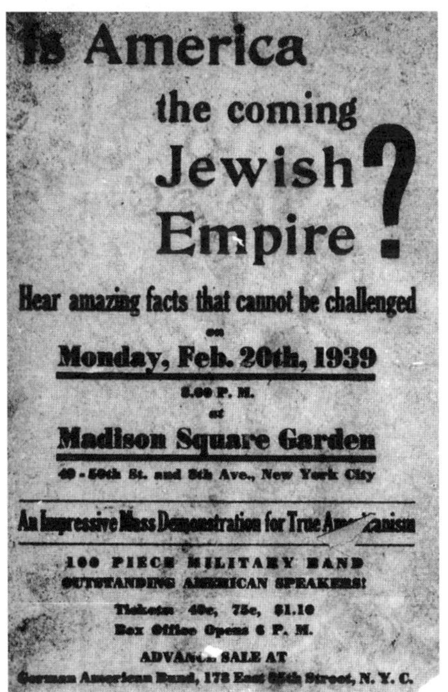

This page: Posters and flyers for the German American Bund's Washington's birthday rally, Madison Square Garden, February 20, 1939. *Fiorello LaGuardia papers, LaGuardia Community College.*

GERMAN AMERICANS! ALL AMERICANS!
STAND UP AGAINST PERSECUTION!

Help Fight the Mad, Infamous Hounding of Fritz Kuhn by the Hate-Blinded, Desperate International Jew and His Politician-Slaves!

The war-mongering international Jew and his creatures are enraged that **the members and sympathizers of the Fighting Movement of the German-blooded Americans have so wonderfully expressed their faith in their Leader and their supreme contempt for his persecutors as to put up the tremendous sum of FIFTY THOUSAND DOLLARS, to cover the outrageous bail under which he is being held!**

And that in the face of the almighty Dewey's charge that Fritz Kuhn "stole" some fourteen thousand dollars from these very members and sympathizers! Isn't it heart-rending to see the unsolicited "concern" being shown by the **Deweys of Jew York** for the safety of the **German American Bund's** money?!

The Bund and its members have absolute faith that ALL of Fritz Kuhn's acts and expenditures have been undertaken in the best interests of the organization and within the powers granted him in 1936, 1937, 1938 and 1939 and specifically reaffirmed each year, despite the insolent charges of meddling politicians with an axe to grind! **Fritz Kuhn is the Bund!**

The "chosen" defenders of the "only true Democracy and Americanism" will be ranting and tearing their hair at the thought that their intended victim is free again to properly prepare his defense; they will be trembling in their boots to find him again free to carry forward the Bund's battle for a CHRISTIAN, NATIONALISTIC and FREE U.S.A., a CONSTITUTIONAL REPUBLIC TRULY INDEPENDENT OF EUROPE, in which the Bill of Rights will apply for the German Element as well as for others! They live in deadly fear of the force of Fritz Kuhn's arguments before the American People! They and the cheap politicians at their beck and call **want him and his co-fighters behind bars, regardless of how this may be achieved! They want him destroyed and his organization blasted!**

Counter-arguments and other honorable methods being unavailing to silence him, Fritz Kuhn's bail may be increased beyond the unheard of sum already set, the increase again being the result of a Jewish assistant district attorney's whispering in a judge's ear! His assistants may be arrested and placed under bond as "material witnesses" or what not (insofar as this has not already been done), so as to further hinder his organized support! We can prepare for everything conceivable which could serve to place an impossible financial load upon his defense!

Bonding firms apparently NOT being free to act in THIS case, CASH must be held available for bail! The entire weight of a political machine apparently being mobilized against the Bund, excellent and capable counsel must be retained! **It is a matter of honor for American Freemen and particularly for the German Element to CONFOUND FRITZ KUHN'S ENEMIES!**

GRANT US LOANS TO COVER BAIL BONDS!
CONTRIBUTE TO THE FIGHTING FUND TO COVER DEFENSE COSTS!
MOVE YOUR FRIENDS AND ACQUAINTANCES TO DO LIKEWISE!

☞ **Telegraph Funds to: WILHELM KUNZE, City Hall Tavern Hall, 754 Palisade Ave., Union City, New Jersey, or deliver them to any Unit Leader of the German American Bund!** ☜

FRITZ KUHN PERSONIFIES THE PERSECUTED GERMAN ELEMENT! HE SHALL WIN!

Free America!

German American Bund

Wilhelm Kunze, National Vice-Leader
August Klapprott, Eastern Department Leader,
George Froboese, Midwestern Department Leader
Hermann Schwinn, Western Department Leader
James Wheeler-Hill, National Secretary
Gustav J. Elmer, National Organizing Director
Willy Luedtke, National Economics Director

Read the "DEUTSCHER WECKRUF UND BEOBACHTER and THE FREE AMERICAN" for truth !

Details and speaker lineup for the German American Bund's Washington's birthday rally. *Fiorello LaGuardia papers, LaGuardia Community College.*

The announcement of the Madison Square Garden rally was met with immediate resistance from anti-fascist groups, labor unions, veterans' groups, the Jewish community, political officials, celebrities, communist groups and concerned citizens alike. In a letter to Mayor LaGuardia, Howard Gordon, a local doctor, argued:

> *I am a firm believer in civil liberties for all, but permitting the Bund members to hold their meeting would not be the extension of the right to assemble, but placing in the hands of a rope to strangle all rights and liberties we as Americans hold dear. Eternal watchfulness is the price of liberty, and now, we must be guarded more than ever.*

In an additional letter of protest from the German-American League for Culture (Deutschamerikanischer Kulturverband), President Otto Sattler stated:

> *Please recognize that the misuse of the German-American name on the part of this Hitler-inspired clique has caused much harm to loyal American citizens of German descent. With its claim to represent the German-American population, the Bund tends to identify millions of loyal citizens with its un-American principles of race hatred and dictatorship. To protect law-abiding German Americans, we protest against this attempted demonstration of fake Americanism.*

Despite all the anti-fascist groups and concerned citizens expressing safety concerns and outrage, Mayor LaGuardia refused to have the city cancel the scheduled rally. In a statement, he said:

> *As long as this meeting is conducted in an orderly and lawful manner with no violence advocated and no preaching the overthrow of this government by violence, it will be permitted to continue. Our government provides free speech, and that right will be respected in this city. It would be a strange kind of free speech that permits free speech for those we agree with. That's the kind of free speech they have in Fascist countries—but it isn't free speech.*[77]

After the mayor's decision not to halt the rally, the "Non-sectarian Anti-Nazi League" filed for counter-protest permits. Fearing a potential riot, LaGuardia stationed 1,700 armed police officers outside Madison Square

American League
FOR PEACE and DEMOCRACY

NEW YORK CITY DIVISION · 112 East 19th Street, New York City · ALGONQUIN 4-9290

DR. HARRY F. WARD
National Chairman

City Executive Committee

ELEANOR BRANNAN
Chairman

REV. DAVID LICORISH
ARTHUR J. MCLAUGHLIN
ISIDORE SORKIN
Vice-Chairmen

HELEN R. BRYAN
Executive Secretary

OSCAR SCHNELLER
Acting Organization Secretary

ALBERT HYMAN
Treasurer

ISRAEL AMTER
MRS. J. X. COHEN
ABRAHAM FEINGOLD
JACOB MIRSKY
CYRIL PHILIP
REV. FREDERICK REUSTLE
KATHERINE TERRILL

Staff

WILLIAM MALES
Legislative

RUTH DOBRER
National Minorities and Race Relations

CYRUS S. PORTER
Campaigns

BRIAN HEALD
MORRIS ENGEL
Education

ANNA C. SCHNEIDERMAN
Women

CLIFFORD WELCH
Publications

GORDON SLOANE
Youth

RAY AVERSA
Trade Union

HERMAN STOLLEY
Anti-Nazi Dept.

ALBERT PRENTIS
Cultural

Advisory Board

PROF. E. B. BURGUM
JOHN CHAMBERLAIN
MALCOLM COWLEY
MARTHA FOLEY
DAVID FREEMAN
REV. WILLIAM LLOYD IMES
MILTON KAUFMAN
VITO MARCANTONIO
REV. A. CLAYTON POWELL, JR.
REV. HERMAN F. REISSIG
ELMER RICE
PROF. MARGARET SCHLAUCH
LEE SIMONSON
PROF. ROBERT K. SPEER
ASHLEY P. TOTTEN
THOMAS YOUNG

FEB 11 1939
IN MAIL ROOM

February 10, 1939.
4005 Sea Gate Ave
Sea Gate, N.Y. Harbor.

Honorable Mayor Fiorella La Guardia,
City Hall,
New York City, N.Y.

My dear Mayor La Guardia,

The German-American Bund is planning to hold a meeting at Madison Square Garden on Monday February 20th.

The Sea Gate branch of the American League for Peace & Democracy, wishes, to raise it's voice in protest against this proposed meeting.

We are fully in accord with the idea that every individual or organization is entitled to the enjoyment of the rights and priviliges guaranteed by the constitution of our land.

The very announcement of this meeting however contradicts everything that is truly American, and it is therefore a fair conclusion that any organization so constituted, may forfeit the rights, which by implication at least, are meant to be employed towards the building up of our institutions not destroying them.

Every true and loyal American deplores the fact that an enterprise such as Madison Square Garden, catering as it does to Citizens of every race, color and creed should open its doors to this openly Anti-Semitic and Nazi minded Bund.

Sincerely yours,

Garden on the evening of the rally, and 600–700 officers were posted inside the venue. On the evening of the rally, over 100,000 people were present, either at the rally, in counterdemonstrations or as spectators. Banners reading "Smash Anti-Semitism" and "Drive the Nazis out of New York" were paraded around the Garden for attendees to see. The lines of people along Eighth Avenue throughout the Bund rally were, for the most part,

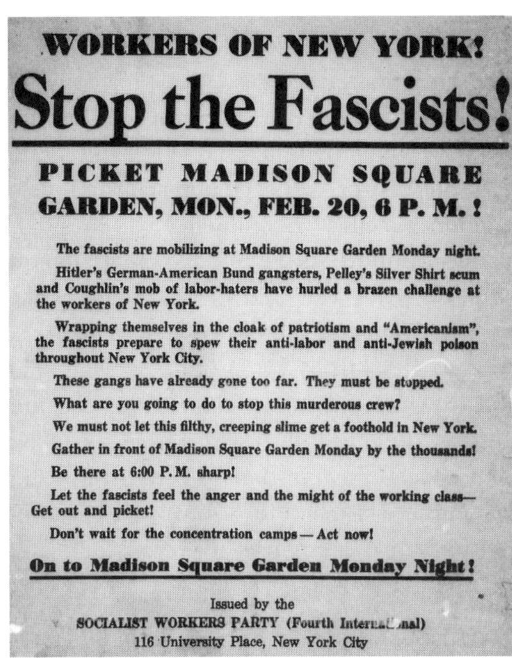

WORKERS OF NEW YORK!

Stop the Fascists!

PICKET MADISON SQUARE GARDEN, MON., FEB. 20, 6 P. M.!

The fascists are mobilizing at Madison Square Garden Monday night.

Hitler's German-American Bund gangsters, Pelley's Silver Shirt scum and Coughlin's mob of labor-haters have hurled a brazen challenge at the workers of New York.

Wrapping themselves in the cloak of patriotism and "Americanism", the fascists prepare to spew their anti-labor and anti-Jewish poison throughout New York City.

These gangs have already gone too far. They must be stopped.

What are you going to do to stop this murderous crew?

We must not let this filthy, creeping slime get a foothold in New York.

Gather in front of Madison Square Garden Monday by the thousands!

Be there at 6:00 P. M. sharp!

Let the fascists feel the anger and the might of the working class—Get out and picket!

Don't wait for the concentration camps—Act now!

On to Madison Square Garden Monday Night!

Issued by the
SOCIALIST WORKERS PARTY (Fourth International)
116 University Place, New York City

Opposite and left: Letter and flyer from the American League for Peace and Democracy and Socialist Workers Party protesting the German American Bund's Washington's birthday rally. *Fiorello LaGuardia papers, LaGuardia Community College.*

peaceful, except for the small groups of anti-Nazi protestors who tried to break through the police barricade to storm the rally inside the Garden.

As guests filed in, kiosks sold Nazi flags, copies of *Mein Kampf* and anti-Semitic radio preacher Father Coughlin's *Social Justice* magazine. The stage at the Garden was decorated with two thirty-foot posters of George Washington, and American flags were displayed on both sides of the stage. In between the American flags and the Washington posters, swastika banners were suspended from the ceiling. Standing at attention on and around the stage were Hitler Youth members and SS soldiers. As people took their seats, a brass band played parade music. Audience members held anti-Semitic signs that read "Stop Jewish domination of Christian America." Bund member Margarete Rittershaus sang "The Star-Spangled Banner" to open the rally, followed by Lutheran minister Sigmund Von Bosse's opening prayers.

Speakers included James Wheeler-Hill, Bund national secretary; Rudolf Markmann, leader of the East Coast branches; George Froboese, leader of the Midwest chapters; Herman Schwinn, leader of the West Coast branches; and Wilhelm Kunze, vice president of the Bund. During Schwinn's speech, he delivered intense criticism of Jewish people immigrating to America, referring to the United States as "Jew-Nited States" and New York as "Jew York." Schwinn ranted against the democratic system of government, stating,

"There is no such thing as Democracy in the United States, and there is no mention of Democracy in the Constitution of our country; however, there is a mention of Republicanism." At the close of his speech, Schwinn declared that the foes of the Bund and Nazism were hiding behind so-called "Democratic ideals" that are not in the Constitution.[78] Kunze's speech detailed the Bund's progress and the importance of fighting against the influence of "President Rosenfeld" (Roosevelt) and his Jewish financiers Henry Morgenthau and Bernard Baruch.

As the speakers took the stage, reporter and anti-fascist activist Dorothy Thompson heckled and laughed at them from her front-row seat. The cheers of fellow Bund members drowned out her disdain. After the first few speakers, Bund SS troopers escorted her out through thousands of Nazi followers name-calling her. Once out of the Garden, she told inquiring counter protesters and other reporters, "I laughed for a purpose. I wanted to demonstrate how perfectly absurd all this defense of free speech is in connection with movements and organizations like this one."[79]

Toward the end of the rally, during Fritz Kuhn's speech, an unemployed Jewish plumber, Isadore Greenbaum, attempted to rush the stage. Bund members tackled and started to beat him; police officers broke up the fight and arrested Greenbaum for disorderly conduct. After Greenbaum was ejected from the rally, Kuhn went on to denounce the "campaign of hate being waged against the organization in the press, radio, and cinema, at the hands of Jews." Kuhn, in closing, demanded members "protect their children and homes from the United States, which is turning into a Bolshevik paradise driven by Jewish communist force."

In total, thirteen counterdemonstrators were arrested on the night of the rally. Isadore Greenbaum, the only person detained inside the Garden, was fined twenty-five dollars. The judge asked, "Do you realize that someone could've been hurt by what you did on stage?" Greenbaum replied, "Don't you realize that someone is going to be hurt by what was being said on stage?"[80] In the months after his arraignment, when he was asked about his actions, Greenbaum stated, "I went down to the Garden without any intention of interrupting, but being that they talked so much against my religion, and there was so much persecution, I lost my head, and I felt it was my duty to talk."

In response to the counterprotests at the rally, Nazi-controlled media ran an article headlined "Jewish Terror in New York and the Battle for a Free America." The article called the protests "a new attempt of Jewry to express its hate and revenge." LaGuardia responded to the Nazi critics in a press release, stating, "I am not at all worried about irresponsible statements of irresponsible governments." New Yorkers' reactions to LaGuardia's decision to allow the rally with tax-funded police protection were not only splashed across newspaper columns but also voiced in letters of disdain from members of the Jewish community. In a letter, a New York City resident named Katherine Warner argued,

> *Why should the right of Free Speech be granted to a group that represents a foreign country in which the right to life, liberty, and the pursuit of happiness has been crushed? Why should we provide police protection and privileges of our country's freedom to a group that works to destroy the structure of our country? Why do we allow them to preach race hatred as Americanism? Perhaps Austria and Czechoslovakia gave the Nazis freedom of Speech too?*

In a letter to his acquaintance, Rabbi Leon Spitz of the American Jewish Congress, LaGuardia defended his handling of the rally, citing his lack of legal options because it was held in a privately owned auditorium that required no mandated city permits. He further argued that police protection was for public safety and not a privilege extended to the Bund.

On February 27, as a direct rebuttal to the Bund rally, the National Communist Party held a rally in Madison Square Garden to celebrate the twelfth anniversary of the founding of the Third International Workers Party. In attendance were twelve thousand communists, who faced no counterprotests outside the Garden. The meeting started by denouncing the New York City police for protecting the Nazi rally. Rally headliners demanded that all members in attendance become more militant in their reaction to fascist groups. Another anti-Nazi proposal was the lobbying of a law to the New York State legislature that made it illegal to wear a Nazi

Pro-Nazi postcard sent to New York City Mayor Fiorello LaGuardia. *Fiorello LaGuardia papers, LaGuardia Community College.*

uniform in public. Within a few months of the rally, a bill sponsored by the New York State majority leader, Republican Joe Hanley, was presented, which would ban wearing any military (if not a member of the armed services) or stormtrooper uniform in public. But despite the support of the majority leader, the rest of the Republican base rejected it due to the Communist Party's support. In a letter to Israel Amter, chairperson of the state Communist Party, Edward Jaeckle, chairman of the state Republican Committee, explained:

> *Relative to your communication endorsing our bill to curb un-American propaganda and demonstrations, may we point out that no organization in this country is more offensive than the Communist Party? If we understand the temper of the present legislature, you may expect equal diligence in suppressing subversive activities on the part of the Communist Party.*[81]

LaGuardia touted the response to the event as a success: the city, he said, was an exemplary model of free speech with little to no violent backlash. Within his inner circle, LaGuardia acknowledged concerns about the potential rise of an American Reich. Preventing another Bund rally in New York City would come with challenges, but legislating rules around public safety for future large-scale rallies, LaGuardia thought, could be an effective roadblock to future large Bund-like events. In a mayoral executive order, LaGuardia declared that leasing halls that provided their own ushers was prohibited. Only licensed police officers wearing their uniforms could be used at these venues, and all approval of large-scale events was pending full approval of the New York City Police Commissioner.

LaGuardia's other goal was to dismantle Kuhn's influence in expanding the Bund. In letters to District Attorney Thomas Dewey, LaGuardia brainstormed potential charges that could be filed against Kuhn. Local chapters of the American Legion had petitioned the U.S. District Attorney's office with complaints that Bund members impersonated armed services members by wearing SS uniforms with United States military accessories. But impersonation charges would be flimsy at best. At LaGuardia's suggestion, Dewey's office started to probe into the Bund's tax documents. These tax documents and the Bund's financial earnings statements would become the smoking gun that would take down Kuhn.

CHAPTER 7

FALL OF KUHN AND THE BUND

On April 30, 1939, Kuhn held his West Coast Americanism Rally, which took place in Hindenburg Park, Los Angeles. Before the rally, Kuhn met with all Bund chapter leaders about the Dies Committee, Dewey's investigation into Kuhn and the New York state legislator's proposed ban on SS uniforms. In conclusion of the meeting, Kuhn gave a directive to all Bund chapters to remain "undercover and not seek the limelight." The only chapters exempt from this order were New York City, Los Angeles and Chicago. All public activities that would give other Bund chapters media exposure must be canceled. At the rally, an estimated 1,200 Bund members representing chapters in Seattle, San Francisco, Oakland, San Diego, Petaluma and Los Angeles were in attendance. West Coast Bund leader Herman Schwinn opened the rally by reading a telegram from the Bund to President Roosevelt. The telegram read, "We demand you do everything in your power to quarantine the United States against alien influences which are at work to drag the nation into war." The keynote speaker that followed was Kuhn, who had a defensive tone, which differed from the tone he took at the Madison Square Garden rally months prior. Kuhn made his speech brief and declared, "The time is past when we German-Americans must ask for our rights—we now demand them. We are not trying to overthrow the government of the United States, but to give Americans of German descent a true understanding of the current problems."

Coming back to New York, Kuhn faced the changing reality of his untouchable sense of security being shaken. Under the direction of Mayor LaGuardia, New York City Commissioner of Investigations William

Herlands found over forty city tax violations committed by Kuhn and the Bund's various corporations. Charges ranged from filing false returns, failing to collect sales tax, failing to register as a vendor and failing to file personal property taxes. The bulk of the investigation stemmed from the Bund not collecting sales tax on swastika emblems, uniforms, pamphlets and other Nazi paraphernalia sold at events, such as the February 20 rally. Named as the main culprits were Fritz Kuhn; Max Rapp, treasurer of the German-American Businessmen's League; William Leudtke, manager of the German-American Businessmen's League; Richard Metten, treasurer of the Bund's publishing company, A.V. Publishing; James Wheeler-Hill, Bund treasurer; Max Buchte, custom tailor of SS uniforms; Karl Kienzler, president of Kienzler and Schimpf Importing Corp.; and Fred Kackal, president of the Bund printing company, Kackal Press.

When the announcement of the investigation was made public, Kuhn and other Bund leaders attempted to get passports but had their applications blocked on LaGuardia's request. By the end of May, Attorney General Dewey had filed an additional indictment against Kuhn for twelve counts of grand theft. The indictment charged Kuhn with embezzling $14,458 from the Bund's general fund. The maximum sentence for a conviction on all counts was thirty years. A portion of the stolen funds, totaling $8,907, came from the proceeds of the February 20 rally in Madison Square Garden. The second-largest amount stolen was $4,424 from the Bund's various corporations, including the German American Settlement League, which owned Camp Siegfried. Before the indictment was announced, Kuhn and three other Bund leaders, Thomas Dixon, Gustave Elmer and Wilhelm Kunze, fled by car into Pennsylvania. While Kuhn was picking up luggage in Krumsville, Pennsylvania, he was arrested by detectives who had followed him from New York. Once detained, Kuhn insisted he would return to enter a plea to the indictment. He said he was not trying to flee law enforcement but was scheduled to give speeches in Chicago and Milwaukee.[82]

Once in custody, Kuhn retained counsel Peter Sabbatino for his defense. He entered a not-guilty plea, and bail was set at $5,000. Once bail was set, Sabbatino moved for a delay in trial scheduling, arguing, "I intend to postpone this defendant's trial because of the community's state of mind, which the newspapers have aroused to the extent that the defendant cannot procure a fair trial." In response to Sabbatino's request, the judge set the trial date for late November. In another legal motion, Kuhn's defense team requested to be furnished with the list of witnesses in the grand jury indictment and the five financial books of the Bund's corporations, which were seized without a proper warrant. The judge denied the request and said it could be revisited during Kuhn's trial.

Kuhn posted bail, and the following day came with concerns of a potential charge from federal authorities. The Dies Commission (House Un-American Activities Committee) had been progressing with its inquiry into Nazi propaganda in the United States. At the top of its focus was the Bund's two official newsletters, *Weckruf und Beobachter* and *The Free American*. Despite all the legal troubles and ongoing investigations, the July Fourth Bund National Convention in Astoria, Queens, was not canceled, and elections were held to reelect Kuhn as national leader. Following the election convention, delegates attended the Siegfried Fourth of July celebration/Kuhn's reelection rally. The event attracted only two thousand people and was presided over by West Coast Bund leader Herman Schwinn. Schwinn gave multiple speeches on the importance of contributing to Kuhn's defense fund. In the aftermath of his reelection, Kuhn went on a public relations blitz, defending himself against the charges and arguing he was the victim of hateful media and the Jewish political machine. At one rally, Kuhn said, "Ten members of Dewey's staff are communists."

As the state trial date drew near and the Dies congressional investigation heated up against the Bund and Kuhn, loyal members started to leave for Germany. Per a direct order from New York District Attorney Thomas Dewey, Kuhn was rearrested and held on $50,000 bail as he was considered a flight risk. Assistant District Attorney Milton Schilback stated, "We have authentic secret information that Kuhn is planning to flee the country and may not be available when his case comes to trial."

Assistant District Attorney Herman McCarthy focused on the so-called führer principle within the Bund: the führer can do with the Bund's funds as he likes; he is responsible to no one but the Bund.[83] McCarthy detailed in court how Kuhn used his power (per the führer principle) to embezzle funds to purchase gifts for his mistress, Florence Camp. Love letters between Camp and Kuhn were read in court, highlighting Kuhn's promises to leave his wife for her and cover some of her living expenses. The money Camp received from Kuhn was traced back to Camp Siegfried's daily operation budget. Additional mismanaged funds discovered during the trial came in the form of bribes to get Camp Siegfried's beer license renewed.

In opening remarks, Kuhn's lawyer argued,

> *The case is a political prosecution to boost District Attorney Thomas Dewey. While I had no respect for the things the Bund represents nor for*

Journalist John Metcalfe at the Dies hearing, demonstrating how he went undercover in the Bund as Hellmut Oberwinder. *Library of Congress.*

Former member of the German Bund Peter P. Gissibl of Chicago testifying before the House Un-American Activities Committee. *Library of Congress.*

> *Kuhn's methods, the man should not be made a martyr. The evidence about Kuhn's affairs is not for the court but for the newspaper boys.*[84]

Disregarding Sabbatino's rebuke, McCarthy further detailed the affair as the trial progressed. Sabbatino then filed an application with the court for a mistrial, claiming that an "unfair and dastardly attack had been made on the defense by McCarthy in summing up the proceedings [related to the affair]." The judge threw out Sabbatino's motion for a mistrial. On November 29, the jury convened for seven and a half hours before requesting a rereading of the specific charge tied to Florence Camp.[85] After half an hour of rereading the charge, they decided on the verdict, returning to the courtroom around ten o'clock in the evening. Kuhn stood as the jury filed back into the room. His expression was blank and calm as Morris Bullock, jury foreman, read the verdict: guilty on five of the twelve counts of grand larceny. National Chairman of the Bund Wilhelm Kunze, who stood by Kuhn throughout the trial, started a fundraiser across all chapters to pay his legal fees and file an appeal. Kunze told all local chapters, "We cannot go on unless large sums of money are available. We will carry this battle through until Kuhn is free again. We will go on till hell freezes."[86]

On December 6, 1939, Kuhn stood before Judge James Wallace for sentencing. Judge Wallace sentenced Kuhn to a suspended sentence related to the charges involving Florence Camp and to two and a half to five years on each of the remaining three accounts, to be served concurrently.[87] After the judge announced the sentencing, Sabbatino declared assertively, "It goes to show what lengths people will go to destroy this defendant." The judge replied, "Don't lose your self-control." The following day, Kuhn, prisoner no. 26558, was shipped to New York's Sing Sing Prison to start his sentence.

On January 3, 1940, the new year brought another indictment against national Bund secretary James Wheeler-Hill, this time for perjury involving his immigration/legalization status. During congressional hearings and court proceedings, Wheeler-Hill said he was born in San Francisco, but in fact, he was born in Latvia, then part of the Russian empire, and was living in America illegally. Because the Bund was quick to hide members' sedition using free speech constitutional guarantees, the legal argument shifted to questioning members' citizenship and to potential denaturalization. If Kuhn and other members of the Bund wanted to be part of the Reich, they could be sent back to Germany. By 1941, the FBI and Immigration and Naturalization Services had begun the process of stripping citizenship from Kuhn and declaring him an enemy alien. Once he was denaturalized, a deportation order followed, which had Kuhn sent from a New York State prison after his sentencing to federal detention due to his enemy alien status. He would be held and deported once America defeated Germany.

Due to Kuhn's imprisonment and the FBI investigations into the Bund's leadership, many of its holding companies collapsed. In an effort to consolidate properties and have a more affordable option for camp operations, Bund leadership considered moving Siegfried fifteen miles west to the Suffolk County town of Wyandanch. The Bund purchased 146 acres of pine barren forest, with a pond. When the Bund petitioned town officials for a permit to build an extensive clubhouse, the Wyandanch community grew concerned that the Bund would move Siegfried to their town. Judge John Clinton Robbins, who was on the town lighting committee and responsible for approving the extension of electric lines, stated:

> *Rumors have reached me that the chief purpose of these light and electricity lines will be for a clubhouse used by the German-American Bund. Protests have been received that the Bund intends to move from Yaphank to Wyandanch, and I, for one, will do nothing to further anything un-American. I object to issuing a certificate of occupancy.*

A Bund developer argued, "You can't do that; the land is used for permanent community housing."[88]

Despite protests from the Bund, it was rejected for a permit. Yaphank would remain home to the Bund but face an uncertain future due to the rising expenses of the property and its declining membership. The Amerika-Deutscher Development Company, one of the many limited liability companies started by the Bund to finance the camp's expansion, split from the Bund and became a separate entity. During the split from the Bund, the company demanded full payment of $5,000 and $1,440 in interest from the German American Settlement League. On June 20, 1941, the development company officially filed foreclosure proceedings on a sixty-acre tract of land that made up the heart of Camp Siegfried.

CHAPTER 8

AMERICA'S NEXT FÜHRER

The Siegfried rallies were not reserved only for the German American Bund but were open to groups with similar ideologies. The Citizens Protection League, Protestant Civic Welfare Association, Christian-Gentile Committee, Christian Defenders, Christian Front, German-American Republican League and National Committee Against Communism were close collaborators of the Bund. The leadership of all these groups worked in sync with Nazi ideology and mobilized collectively for large-scale rallies. The most significant impact of these pro-Nazi/fascist rallies was the rise of several cult-like personalities competing to be the next American führer to replace Fritz Kuhn. Through a series of legal indictments, Fritz Kuhn and other Bund leaders lost their grip on power over the New York fascist movement. This created a power vacuum to be filled by another führer to lead America's fascist movement.

A top contender who would be able to bridge all of New York State's fascist groups was Edward James Smythe. In his early years, Smythe's reputation was marred with multiple charges of grand larceny and assault. In 1927, Smythe became interested in politics and volunteered for New York State Governor Al Smith's presidential campaign. During this time, he familiarized himself with the ins and outs of campaign pamphlets and mailings and their ability to sway public opinion. Rising within the volunteer ranks, he took charge of the monthly Democratic Party journals *The Democratic Review*, *The Political Digest* and *The Democratic Biography*. He was arrested in 1928 for falsely advertising these journals as direct endorsements of the National Democratic Party and

The fall of Fritz Kuhn led to multiple fascist groups competing for Bund membership. *Nassau County Photograph Archive.*

illegally soliciting fees for advertisement space. Following his arrest, Smythe switched sides and became a supporter of Herbert Hoover for president and a Republican Party member. While out on bail, he created another journal/daily bulletin, marketed as a product of the official National Hoover for President League, and illegally sold advertisement space. The New York

City Police arrested him again and revoked his bail. While in custody, he had a psychiatric episode and was committed to Bellevue Psychiatric Hospital for observation.[89]

In the aftermath of his legal troubles, Smythe became obsessed with the rising fascist movements. His first move toward establishing an American fascist movement was founding the Protestant War Veterans Organization, which was affiliated with the Ku Klux Klan. These two groups operated with the unified goal of expanding their ideology and influence instead of competitive membership. The unified Klan and Protestant War Veterans membership focused on anti-Jewish, anti-Catholic and anti-Roosevelt messaging. This helped Smythe establish a base to preside over and allowed the Klan to establish a limited liability corporation (LLC) under a different name (it was banned from forming an LLC using the Klan name in New York and Georgia).

Smythe further expanded his influence by creating a working partnership with the Independent Republican National Christian-Gentile Committee. This partnership allowed Smythe to use the organization's printing/distribution and lobbying resources for Klan and Protestant War Veterans operations. The unified coalition endorsed and advocated for former Pennsylvania Congressman Louis McFadden, whom other congressmen criticized for his multiple speeches blaming the Great Depression on Jewish bankers. Using this political momentum, Smythe expanded his coalition by merging the Protestant Civic Welfare Association and the National Committee Against Communism and assuming the role of chairman. Once these four groups had been brought together with the allied New York State Klan, he influenced the flow of propaganda to their members through weekly newsletters. Using the German American Bund rallies as a launch pad to grow his following and form an alliance with other established paramilitary groups, Smythe became a frequent guest at all Bund meetings and summer camp events. At his first speech to the four unified groups, during the German American Bund New York City town hall rally on March 15, 1937, Smythe declared:

> *The International Jewish Cliques rewrote the constitution of the Republic of Germany, jammed it down 68 million German Christians, and enslaved them economically, socially, and politically. They are trying to do the same here, but they will find us a much harder job because when the one hundred and twenty million Christians awaken, the bloody purge of Hitler will look like a picnic.*[90]

As Smythe's influence expanded, he finalized a partnership between the New York State Klan and the German American Bund during the Bund's 1940 annual conference at Camp Nordland, New Jersey. The agreement was styled as a military alliance between the two groups for what the Bund members called the Tag (the day they would rise up, overthrow the government and establish an American Reich). At the close of the meeting, Smythe said, "The heart of every true crusading American is in the cell with your incarcerated leader, Fritz Kuhn, whom I am proud to call my friend."[91]

Spawned from the hate preached at German Bund meetings and by Father Charles Coughlin, Joe McWilliams was a secondary contender to be America's next führer. McWilliams had rebranded himself, transforming from an aspiring engineer with strong Marxist leanings into a far-right, anti-Semitic, anti-Communist, pro-Nazi demagogue-like character. Given the nickname Joe McNazi by radio personality Walter Winchell, McWilliams became active in the Father Coughlin–inspired group Christian Mobilizers (the group was an extension of Coughlin's other paramilitary group, Christian Front). By 1939, he had built a strong base in the Christian Mobilizers and assumed leadership over the city chapters. Under his leadership, he toured around New York City's densely populated German communities to expand the Mobilizers' membership rolls.

McWilliams attempted to run for Congress in the city's Eighteenth Congressional District as a Republican. He would have a platform equipped with a spotlight assembled for his stump speeches, with which he would spotlight hecklers and have them removed from the crowd.[92] During his firebrand speeches, he would state that New York Governor Herbert Lehman was a "Jew" and New York City Mayor Fiorello LaGuardia was a "Jew parading under an Italian name." During these speeches and rallies, McWilliams would invite Chief New Moon, a frequent guest of the Bund at Camp Siegfried. Thomas Dixon, who was of Cherokee descent, referred to himself as Chief New Moon and argued in favor of "Hitler's warrior culture" and historical connections between Native Americans and the swastika.[93] In one speech hosted by McWilliams and the Christian Mobilizers, New Moon stated, "The Jews controlled the United States, and they were running the government, despite crying they are a minority. Imagine just how much control they would have if they were a majority."[94] Furthering McWilliams's influence were the estimated four hundred officers of the New York City Police Department who were known members of the Christian Front or the Christian Mobilizers. His growing base and influence did not sway the local Republican Party to endorse him for the Eighteenth Congressional

District election. In response to not being endorsed, McWilliams created the American Destiny Party with the support of the Bund. The Bund held rallies for the Destiny Party at its Yorkville headquarters and Camp Siegfried, drawing thousands of pro-fascist, anti-Semitic, racist individuals and groups with the appeal of unifying under one political party. Henry Curtis, a supporter of the Destiny Party, created a weekly newsletter named *Curtis Weekly American Bulletin*, in which he republished McWilliams's speeches and furthered conspiracy theories about how local, state and federal government power was held in the hands of Jews who wanted to take the United States into a war against Christians.

O. John Rogge served as the assistant attorney general in Franklin Roosevelt's administration. During his career, he was the federal prosecutor for what was known as the Great Sedition Trial. *Library of Congress.*

Despite the push in support from the Bund community and its affiliates, McWilliams lost his bid in his newly established party due to being disqualified from the general election. By 1943, the reorganized groups under Smythe and his Bund partnership had started to fall apart. In an interview, Smythe stated,

> *Remember that joint meeting between the Klan and the Bund at Camp Nordland in New Jersey? I organized that and was supposed to get a 25 percent cut. I took in over $5,000, by God, and I never got a dime.*[95]

But the full demise of Edward James Smythe and Joe "McNazi" McWilliams came in 1944 through a federal indictment for violating the Smith Act (which made advocating, teaching or advising anything related to the destruction of the United States illegal). Both men, prior to the indictments, were flagged by the FBI as Nazi propagandists, along with twenty-eight other suspects who had ties to or were loosely associated with the Nazi government. After the initial arraignment, Smythe stated, "The charges were based on political gossip of Walter Winchell."[96] During their trial (known as the Great Sedition Trial), District Attorney John Rogge laid out his case before presiding Judge Edward Eicher for over eleven months until Judge Eicher died on November 30, 1944. Due to the judge's untimely death, a mistrial was declared, and

DEPARTMENT OF JUSTICE
WASHINGTON, D.C.

OJR:e

January 24, 1944

AIR MAIL

Mr. Joseph Roos
727 West 7th Street
Los Angeles, California

Re: United States v. McWilliams

Dear Mr. Roos:

At the trial of this case, which I hope will begin in March, I intend to use as witnesses Roy H. Arnold and Charles J. Young, both of whom turned in reports to you. If you have copies of their reports I would like you to send them to me immediately so that I may prepare their testimony for trial.

Federal Bureau of Investigation reports refer to your Informant B. I would like to know whether this Confidential Informant is available to testify and, if so, his name and address.

With best wishes I remain

Very sincerely,

O. John Rogge

O. JOHN ROGGE, Special Assistant
to the Attorney General

A memo to Joseph Roos related to Joe "McNazi" McWilliams being charged as a defendant in the Great Sedition Trial. *Northridge University Library, Digital Collections.*

the defendants were cleared of all charges. Getting off through a mistrial cleared them of criminal charges, but their base of followers eroded due to neglect and changing popular views spurred by World War II. Establishing a following of the size and at the speed McWilliams and Smythe did was made possible by a long-ingrained propaganda machine and enablers at the highest levels of government. As the media covered their trial, journalists redirected their focus to disturbing revelations about trusted elected officials who swore to uphold the Constitution but conspired with Germany to undermine the United States.

CHAPTER 9

NAZI PROPAGANDA MACHINE

"Getting the Bang for Your Buck"

In the aftermath of Heinz Spanknoebel being indicted and recalled to Germany, Nazi leadership shifted its methods of delivering and marketing propaganda. Building German-friendly organizations would no longer be the centerpiece of their efforts to sway the United States support toward the Nazis. According to a 1940 Massachusetts Institute of Technology study on American public opinion and World War II, 67 percent of Americans stated that it should be a priority to help England by any means necessary, and 33 percent stated it was important for Americans to stay neutral or out of the war altogether. Adding to the one-third of Americans wanting an isolationist policy, Congress became sharply divided, not along party lines but between supporters and detractors of Roosevelt. American-based German-friendly clubs would have to have the indirect support of the Nazis, and propaganda efforts would be needed to expand the percentage of Americans who wanted to remain neutral. According to a study conducted by Director of Strategic Services William Donovan and Secretary of the Navy William Franklin Knox, throughout the 1930s, the Nazi government spent an estimated $200 million on propaganda abroad. In a series of articles about the Nazi reliance on propaganda, Donovan wrote,

> *Nazi Germany is not a government—not even a folkdom of the sort Nazi orators talk about. Nazi Germany itself is a conspiracy. Its scope is universal, and its aim is world dominion. Its primary agents are the millions of Germans abroad, as they can be induced or compelled to serve a German fatherland.*[97]

Donovan warned that members of Nazi organizations in the United States were being trained in arms in case America declared war on Germany. However, the FBI and American officials overlooked the potential impact of Germany having four to five times as many accredited diplomatic and consular agents in each foreign post as any other country.[98] In his report, which the FBI overlooked, Donovan referred to these agents and diplomats as being focused on the highest levels of power throughout the United States.

Donovan's assessment was confirmed after the war through the recovery of cables between Dr. Hans Thomsen, head of the German embassy in Washington, D.C., and Berlin's Nazi Foreign Affairs Office. The cables described a proposed implicit pro-Nazi persuasion media campaign referred to as "well-camouflaged lightning propaganda." Some cables highlighted a request for (and receipt of) $20,000 to promote and publish five isolationist novels and help sway the tone of articles in *Reader's Digest*. Various novels were distributed by New York–based publishing group William C. Lengel and New Jersey–based Flanders Hall, which sold tens of thousands of pro-Nazi books. Berlin used part of the $20,000 for *Reader's Digest*'s hiring of editor Lawrence Dennis and George Eggleton of the Nazi-subsidized magazine *Scribner's Commentator*.[99] Once the magazine employed Dennis and Eggleton, their salaries were not paid directly by *Reader's Digest* but through a public relations agent named Pendleton Dudley. Payment done through a third party was unusual for hired writers and editors within *Reader's Digest*. Senior editor Paul Palmer, who supervised Dennis and Eggleton, had an established relationship with Thomsen. During a congressional hearing related to Nazi propaganda, Thomsen stated: "Paul Palmer and I met several times in Washington, D.C., for lunch. He made a great impression on me and seemed to be a special admirer of Germany, and he wanted to engage in some activity."[100] The friendly relationship with the German embassy influenced Palmer to overlook Dennis's suppression of stories related to Nazi atrocities and redirected the magazine's focus on articles that attacked Vice President Henry Wallace.

Palmer's rapport with Thomsen and other German officials led to his sharing information about corporate publishing with them. An example of this information was when Palmer notified Dennis that he was getting rid of his interest in the *American Mercury* magazine. Dennis advised German officials that "it would be a good opportunity for the Nazis to obtain possession of a magazine of their own."[101] Between 1939 and 1941, Nazi propagandists paid an additional $70,000 to $120,000 in expenses to publish various books.[102] The most circulated books included *We Must Save the Republic* and anti-British books like *The 100 Famines That Rule the British Empire*, *The Hapless Boers*, *Democracy on the Nile* and *Lord Lothian vs. Lord Lothian*. These titles were published by Flanders Hall Publishing, which Nazi agent George Sylvester Viereck managed. Viereck chose from various manuscripts (mainly from Germany) that he thought were critical of "egotistic" British foreign policy and determined which would sell well in the United States.[103] If Viereck believed a given book was a financial risk for Flanders Hall, he requested funding from Germany to compensate for potential losses.[104]

The German embassies in New York and Washington, D.C., had a budget of $3.65 million, funded by the Nazis between 1938 and 1941. This money was allocated for propaganda publications, the influence of elected officials and image-building campaigns for Nazi Germany. Colin Ross, an agent and paid propagandist, wrote to Nazi Minister of Foreign Affairs Joachim von Ribbentrop on August 31, 1938:

> *It would be particularly effective to plant with the opponents of Roosevelt the slogan that Roosevelt, to be re-elected to a third term, would be willing to go to war.*[105]

Measuring the effectiveness of the propaganda and political smear campaigns was the duty of the Vertrauenmaenner/Vertraunebsleute, or simply V-Men. These confidential Nazi agents were stationed in or near German embassies and usually were United States citizens. They were tasked with sampling public opinion and gathering intelligence.[106] The so-called Borchers Telegram, sent on May 13, 1941, was discovered in a raid by law enforcement of the German embassy in New York. The Justice Department ordered the raid due to the embassy's suspected ties to the Abwehr. Hans Borchers, the German consul general in New York, sent the coded telegram to Berlin. The telegram elaborated on an agent named Dinter, who relayed information gathered at a dinner party with an American general and members of Congress to Borchers. Discussed at the dinner was the possibility of America entering the war in Europe and the interest in deploying American troops into Iceland and Greenland.[107]

However, the first test of the lightning propaganda campaign was the 1940 Republican National Convention in Philadelphia. The Nazis' objective was to have the convention adopt an isolationist platform and to disrupt the nomination of pro-interventionist presidential candidate Wendell Willkie. Hans Thomsen proposed a two-part plan to the Nazi foreign affairs office, along with requests for money for each part. The first part was to utilize the fifty isolationist Republican members of Congress to work on the delegates, convincing them to adopt an isolationist platform. The total cost of part one would be $3,000. The second part was an advertisement blitz: publish full-page ads in newspapers in the run-up to the Republican convention "with a very impressive appeal to keep America out of the war." The total cost of part two would range from $60,000 to $80,000.[108]

Thomsen noted in his cable that his Republican friends would cover half of the plan's costs and that Berlin should cover the other half. One of the advertisements funded by Berlin was a two-page spread on June 25, 1940. The spread read:

> *To the delegates of the Republican National Convention and to American mothers, wage earners, Farmers, and Veterans. Stop the March to War. Stop the interventionists and the warmongers. Stop the Democratic Party, which we believe is the war party in the United States and is leading us to a war against the will of the American People.*[109]

The bottom of the advertisement quoted various anti-interventionist senators and was signed by the Committee to Keep America Out of Foreign Wars. This committee got its funding from Berlin for advertisements, but its leadership was presided over by U.S. House of Representatives Foreign Relations Chair Hamilton Fish III of New York.[110]

On the eve of the Pearl Harbor attack, over two dozen members of Congress had ties to Nazi agents, who actively influenced them to advocate for neutrality with Germany and its allies. In New York, Congressman Fish was successfully targeted by the Nazi propaganda machine. Long before he was elected to Congress, his family had established itself as a New York political dynasty since the formation of the United States. Nicolas Fish, great-grandfather of Hamilton Fish III, was the adjutant general for the Second New York Regiment from 1776 through 1786 and fought in the Revolutionary War. His son Hamilton Fish became the sixteenth governor of New York State, and his son Hamilton Fish II represented New York's Twenty-First Congressional District. Continuing the family legacy, Hamilton Fish III first gained notoriety for leading the all-Black unit, the Harlem Hellfighters (369th Infantry Unit), into the Western Front during World War I. Under his leadership, the 369th would be awarded the Croix de Guerre for valor. While in command of the all-Black unit, Fish became known as an advocate for his men against racial discrimination. In the aftermath of the war, Fish was elected to represent the district encompassing Franklin

After a House Rules Committee session, the press interviewed Representative Hamilton Fish on his neutrality. He told reporters that his opponents wanted a new rule created permitting the House to decide policy on three questions: the arms embargo; loans under the cash and carry provision; and the presidential power to determine combat areas—which Fish said were equivalent to giving authority to name an aggressor. *Library of Congress.*

Roosevelt's Hyde Park residence in Dutchess County, New York. He sponsored legislation to create the Tomb of the Unknown Soldier in his first term. In his second term, in 1922, Fish became the first member of Congress to introduce a resolution endorsing a Jewish national homeland in British-mandated Palestine. Fish would go further to declare that "one can be a good American citizen and a Zionist at the same time."[111]

But Fish's legacy as a congressman and his service to his country became defined by his disdain for President Roosevelt, his hate for communists and his nefarious connections to Nazi propaganda agents. During his fifth term in the House of Representatives, the country was in the midst of the Great Depression, the worst economic crisis in American history. Fish focused on the potential threat of a communist overthrow of the United States due to the country's financial vulnerabilities. He formed the Special Committee to Investigate Communist Activities in the United States, known as the Fish Committee, whose main objective was to examine the relationship between the Soviet Union's Communist International and America's Communist Party. The Fish Committee found that there were an estimated 500,000 to 600,000 active communists in America. Fish and his committee analyzed voting trends in Germany and became alarmed at the 4.5 million votes that Communist Party candidates received. Using the German voting statistics, Fish argued that American communists could grow into an even larger voting bloc. Fish attributed the expansion of support for communism in Germany to that country's recognition of the Soviet government and proposed that the United States exclude itself from any trade or market associated with the Soviet Union. Fish's additional proposals included evaluating communist leaders' immigration status for a potential mass deportation. Seeing the rise of the Nazi Party in Europe, Fish came to view it as a viable source of resistance to the perceived communist threat. The nature of Fish's first contact with Nazi agents is unknown. But his relationship with Friends of New Germany member and paid Nazi propaganda agent George Viereck has been confirmed through various testimonies and investigations.

Viereck was paid an estimated $800 ($18,000 today) per month for his service as a Nazi agent. His monthly stipend was paid by a third party, Nazi agent Carl Byoir, who was directly associated with the German Tourist Bureau. Nazi propaganda diversified its focus from implicit pro-Nazi influence to exacerbating political divides. In that vein, Viereck would be tasked with writing speeches for members of Congress who were isolationists and providing abundant pro-Nazi literature to the members of Congress and their districts. After meeting Viereck in 1938, Fish was the keynote speaker at the annual German Day event hosted by the German Bund. He gave a passionate speech about German Americans' many contributions and the importance of the United States staying neutral while standing under a giant swastika. The following year, Fish flew to Germany and met with Nazi Minister of Foreign Affairs Joachim von Ribbentrop about the Nazis' aggressive territorial expansion. After their meeting, Fish stated that Germany's claims were just.[112] Other Nazi connections included Fish renting his New York City home out to a Nazi diplomat for well above market price.[113]

The other isolationist members of Congress sought to attach themselves to something that would appear to be a legitimate political organization with like-minded views. The America First Committee, established in September 1940 by Robert Stuart, a Yale University law student, became a driving force for a noninterventionist platform. The committee's origins had no direct ties to Nazi propaganda or agents. The first national chairman was

Robert E. Wood, a brigadier general during World War I who fought on the Western Front. Wood's firsthand experiences of the horrors of a global war guided his activity in the committee. Many of its founding members, such as future president Gerald Ford, were antiwar students and not defenders of Hitler. But as the group built a strong base, Nazi sympathizers, anti-Semitic groups, pro-fascist groups and the group of elected officials steered by Nazi agents became vocal supporters. Within a short time, the America First Committee became the leading advocate for noninterventionism, employing the charismatic spokesman Charles Lindbergh. In 1938, two years before Lindbergh became a spokesman for the committee, he was invited to Germany to provide his input on the German Luftwaffe fleet. After his visit, Hermann Göring awarded him the Service Cross of the German Eagle. After Lindbergh's visit to Germany, the America First Committee's membership expanded to an estimated eight hundred thousand people, and it wielded political influence locally and federally. Nazi agents' direct role in the establishment of America First was not as tangible as their influence on its members and political allies.

Politically, Long Island was a Republican stronghold that opposed Roosevelt. Many rising stars in the party courted the voter base during state primaries and general elections. Fish and other members of Congress were among the divided Republican and Democratic Parties, hoping to unify both isolationist members, regardless of party, into an anti-Roosevelt referendum. They went on speaking tours promoting a noninterventionist agenda and proclaiming that they were being forced into silence through the intimidation of the media and hostile members of the Roosevelt coalition. The Nassau County chapters of the America First Committee in Five Towns, Freeport, Hicksville and Valley Stream hosted the pro-Nazi members of Congress on their speaking tours. In the early spring of 1941, Freeport organized a 1,600-person rally for the committee in the Freeport High School auditorium. Guest speaker Republican Senator Gerald Nye of North Dakota called on the audience to do "all in your power to prevent the proposed assignment of American warships to convoy duty." He declared that "this is nothing but madness" and "the British Navy was the only navy in history that consistently practiced aggression."[114]

In the coming months, all the New York metro area branches of the America First Committee organized a Madison Square Garden rally to increase influence and membership. This rally attracted only an estimated ten thousand people. According to an analysis of the attendees, 60 percent of them were members of the German American Bund or had attended the 1939 Bund rally on Washington's birthday. In response to the Nazi-supporting audience, booking halls and stadiums for future events became more challenging. As in the case of restrictions against pro-Nazi groups, the Brooklyn Dodgers refused to grant permission for an America First rally at Ebbets Field.[115] America First retaliated by boycotting any organization, such as the Dodgers, that refused to rent their stadium and hall.

In an attempt to distance itself from pro-Nazism, America First refined its message as anti-war propaganda and waged an anti-interventionist campaign against the media. Its agenda was refocused to target so-called pro-war propaganda in public theaters. A letter was sent to all members following the Madison Square Garden rally.

> *All members in each town and village had to check and report on all newsreels, feature films, and shorts running in all Nassau County theaters to determine the extent to which propaganda favors the entrance into war. Members are instructed to document the specific titles and how often each theatre lends itself to this type of propaganda.*[116]

Building on the America First momentum among isolationists, Congressman Fish took a more aggressive tone toward the media's reporting on the expanding war in Europe. In a rebuttal to *New York Times* articles that claimed America was already in the war, Fish said during a town hall debate with his opponent, Adams Shattuck:

> The New York Times *and* The New York Herald Tribune *are insistent that we are in a war. No shot has been fired; no American has been killed; no ship has been sunk. Congress has not declared war, and not fifty members would vote for war. Yet, they try to tell us that we are in the war.*

A woman in the audience questioned Fish's assessment of the conflict. Fish replied: "You women if you believe everything or fifty percent of what you read in the Eastern newspapers or hear over the radio, you ought to look under the bed every night to see if some Jap or Nazi is lurking there."[117]

The town hall meetings and isolationist rallies sponsored by America First met resistance from many religious fellowship groups. The evolving news coming out of Europe provided an opportunity to make Long Island a battleground over support of intervention, despite being a traditional Republican stronghold that did not support Roosevelt. During a religious fellowship rally held at Adelphi University, attended by four hundred people,

Rabbi Stephen Wise stated: "We will not become isolationists despite all the Wheelers, the Nyes and Lindberghs. There is within us an imperishable quality that will defy and outlive a thousand Hitlers." Other speakers, such as Canon Charles W.F. Smith of the National Cathedral in Washington, D.C., critiqued the events in Europe: "The destiny of the immortal soul and all that we cherish are being threatened."

In an effort to shift local perspectives, Mayors William Ross of Lynbrook, Hamilton Gaddis of Malverne, Edward Talfor of East Rockaway and Henry Waldinger of Valley Stream formed the Four Town Committee to Defend America and Aid the Allies. The leaders in these four communities, who opposed the national figures descending on the surrounding towns, had the foresight to understand that a war was inevitable. Their communities would prepare for mobilization before a declaration of war. Valley Stream would roll out one of the most significant mobilization efforts by assisting the civilian aircraft company Columbia Corp in transitioning to almost exclusively military amphibious planes. In the committee's first annual meeting, Defend America leader and local judge Norman Lent told a packed high school gymnasium, "Hitler's word is worthless, and he plans on destroying America and can do so unless England beats him." In closing, he stated, "For years, I campaigned against President Roosevelt and his policies, but this is the time to forget about politics and remember only that we are Americans."

At the federal level, political insiders who were isolationists fought the efforts of all interventionists on Capitol Hill. George Hill, assistant to Congressman Fish and employed with constituent services, had a well-established relationship with Nazi agent George Viereck. During one meeting with Fish, Hill was introduced to Viereck and asked to give him access to Fish's congressional mailing list, which would later be used to mail Nazi-approved propaganda. These mailings aimed to influence people within Fish's district and the surrounding swing districts to adopt a neutral or anti-interventionist view of European events.[118] Nazi-approved material mailed out (with the postage funded by taxpayers, courtesy of Fish) included pamphlets that advertised the main points of the *Protocols of the Elders of Zion*. The massive mailings of Nazi propaganda with his office return address did not alert any ethics committees on Capitol Hill. However, the anti-Nazi organization Fight for Freedom Committee contacted various media outlets to put pressure on authorities to open an investigation. In response to the accusation of mailing Nazi propaganda, Fish stated:

> *I do not know who could have used envelopes bearing my congressional frank* [a privilege allowing Congress members to send official mail without paying postage]. *It certainly was not done by any friend but rather by an enemy trying to smear my name. Perhaps by a member of Fight for Freedom or by a fanatical Jew who is opposed to my fighting against America's entrance into the war.*[119]

Fish's rebuttal to the accusations and the growing media attention would become the center of a congressional hearing in the summer of 1941. Months earlier, George Viereck was indicted under the Foreign Agents Registration Act for not registering as a foreign agent. All his contacts within Congress were being investigated. Hamilton Fish's aide, George Hill, was questioned in one of the many investigative inquiries. Hill denied that he or anyone else in Fish's office had ever come in contact with Viereck or met with him. On October 24, 1941, a government prosecutor, William Powers Maloney, indicted Hill for perjury after proving that Hill and Fish had conversed directly with Viereck. In a press conference, Maloney stated, "The secretary [Hill] was the key man in Washington in the distribution of literature under congressional franks. This was a plan masterminded by German agents."[120]

Hill retained former Westchester County Democratic Congressman John Joseph O'Connor as his lawyer. O'Connor, like Fish, was a vocal anti-interventionist and cochaired the Committee to Keep America Out of Foreign Wars with Fish. At the bail hearing, Maloney disclosed to the judge that Hill had received $12,000 within five months, which was suspected to have been from the German government. Additional testimony led to the discovery of papers from various members of Congress, half burned in an alley near Fish's congressional office in D.C. The presiding judge, Alan Goldsborough, set Hill's bail at $5,000, which was paid for by sympathetic members of Congress.[121] While Hill was out on bail, Maloney subpoenaed franked mail from Fish's office. Hill, in response, moved eight mailbags containing franked mailings approved by Viereck from Fish's office to a personal storeroom.[122] Despite covering up the franked mailings and vocal support from members of his party, who declared his arrest as political retribution from Roosevelt, in January 1942, Hill was sentenced to two years and six months in prison for perjury. Fish, in a press conference related to Hill's sentencing, stated, "I am very sorry to learn that George Hill, a disabled, decorated veteran of World War I and a clerk in my office, has been convicted of perjury. He had an obsession with our involvement in war."[123] When questions about his legal responsibility were raised, Fish responded by threatening lawsuits against journalists who covered the congressional franking story. He singled out Drew Pearson, who wrote the Washington Merry-Go-Round political column in the *Washington Herald.* A month into his sentence, Hill contacted Maloney and asked to give a statement reversing his initial testimony. Hill, in his statement, said:

> *Mr. Fish introduced Viereck to me and told me that 125,000 copies of a speech entitled "Six Men and War" were to be mailed to persons on our mailing list under Senator Ernest Lundeen's frank* [postage]. *I was only the intermediary.*[124]

Viereck wrote the speech "Six Men and War," which was approved by the German government. Minnesota Senator Lundeen, implicated in the mailing scandal, had most of his speeches written by Viereck. Further testimony revealed that Viereck's New York apartment, at which he hosted many elected officials, had a portrait of Hitler on the wall.

The Nazi influence over Fish's isolationist platform and the arrest of Hill would create resistance within Fish's party. Fish's biggest and most vocal critic within his party was state district attorney and future New York governor Thomas Dewey. Dewey, a rising star in the New York State Republican Party, usually kept his criticism of his colleagues to himself. But his once cordial relationship with Fish ended in May 1942, after the depths of his relationship with Nazi agents were made public. During a party leadership meeting at Laurels County Club in Monticello, New York, state Republicans addressed how to manage the growing concern of Nazi influence on policy and resources within their ranks. When members asked Dewey his thoughts on the Nazi influence on policy, they expected him to take a neutral stance because he was competing for his party's nomination as a candidate for governor. Dewey replied, "I will not take the middle of the road. I am against Fish not only for his views but because of the misuse of his office and the associates he had."[125] In the aftermath of the meeting, Fish met with Dewey in an attempt to persuade him to retract his statement and prevent a divide within the party. Dewey would have the meeting transcribed word for word due to his lack of trust in Fish and his associates.

> **Fish:** *I called to say I hope you will not come out against me. I think I can be nominated and elected easily this time. Some of the delegates within the party I have been speaking with said you will try to defeat a soldier, and the war is on. I would hate to do this because I am for you. I told the*

congressman from Long Island and the national committee to tell you. I shall run as a noninterventionist ticket. If there is interference, I would not run as an independent up here [within my district] *but will run as an independent for governor. 80% of people want to stay out of war, and 10% want to get in.*
DEWEY: *This is not a personal matter. Your office was used by our enemies. Our enemies used your congressional office.*
FISH: *There wasn't a word of truth to that. My frank was never used. They sent these mailings outside my office. Everything reported in the* Tribune *is a direct lie. My people up here understand, and I shall get the biggest vote I ever got. I am worried about outside interference. Interference in your run for governor. If you attack a veteran, my friends would go to bat, and I would run myself.*
DEWEY: *That is about as complete a case of blackmail as I have heard. You are calling me to tell me that if I come out for governor and against you, you will run against me and accuse me of being in a political campaign when I ought to be in your army—that is blackmail.*[126]

In the fallout, some members of Dewey's party supported his stance against Fish. One of Dewey's allies was Otto Schuler. Schuler was a former member of the New York City Board of Aldermen, commander of the Elmhurst-Jackson Heights American Legion Post and founder of the German Steuben Club of Queens, which took an anti-Nazi stand. Schuler would become chairman of the Queens Independent Committee for Dewey and focus on delivering central Queens to Dewey in his campaign for governor. Independent voters would be essential for Dewey in the 1942 election due to his very public falling-out with Fish, which turned hard-liners within his party against him.

Thomas Dewey, New York City prosecutor and district attorney in the 1930s and early 1940s and, later, governor of New York. *Library of Congress.*

Dewey's stance against Fish reflected the changing public opinion of Germany. In early September 1941, a Gallup poll found that 74 percent of Americans agreed that "if the United States was to be a free democratic country, the Nazi government in Germany must be destroyed."[127] Dewey would harness this change in sentiment and win the election with over 52 percent of the vote, with Schuler delivering a majority for central Queens.

By 1944, the Justice Department had appointed Special Prosecutor O. John Rogge following the arrest and testimony of Hill and the McCormack-Dickstein Committee's findings on Nazi influence over elected officials' congressional mailings. During Rogge's public court proceedings, Fish's name was constantly evoked in witness testimonies, which put him on the defensive in his district.

Inspired by the public findings and the attempted prosecution of the Nazi agents who worked with the anti-interventionist and isolationist members of Congress, Woody Guthrie wrote the popular song "Mister Charlie Lindbergh." On Guthrie's return after serving as a merchant mariner in the Mediterranean Sea in July 1944, the song grew in popularity in time for the election cycle of 1944. The lyrics read:

Mister Charlie Lindbergh he flew to old Berlin.
Got 'im a big Iron Cross, and he flew right back again
To Washington, Washington.

Mrs. Charlie Lindbergh she come dressed in red.
Said: "I'd like to sleep in that pretty White House bed
In Washington, Washington."

Lindy said to Annie: "We'll get there by and by,
But we'll have to split the bed up with Wheeler, Clark, and Nye
In Washington, Washington."

Hitler wrote to Lindy said, "Do your very worst."
Lindy started an outfit that he called America First
In Washington, Washington.

All around the country, Lindbergh he did fly.
Gasoline was paid for by Hoover, Clark, and Nye
In Washington, Washington.

Lindy said to Hoover: "We'll do the same as France.
Make a deal with Hitler, and then we'll get our chance.
In Washington, Washington."

Then they had a meetin', and all the Firsters come,
Come on a-walkin, they come on a-runnin'
In Washington, Washington.

Yonder comes Father Coughlin, wearin' the silver chain,
Cash on his stomach and Hitler on the brain
In Washington, Washington.

Mister John L. Lewis would sit and straddle a fence.
His daughter signed with Lindbergh, and we ain't seen her since
In Washington, Washington.

Hitler said to Lindy: "Stall 'em all you can.
Gonna bomb Pearl Harbor with the help of old Japan."
In Washington, Washington.

Then, on a December mornin', the bombs come from Japan.
Wake Island and Pearl Harbor killed fifteen hundred men.
In Washington, Washington.

Now Lindy tried to join the army, but they wouldn't let 'im in,
'Fraid he'd sell to Hitler a few more million men.
In Washington, Washington.

So I'm a-gonna tell you people: If Hitler's gonna be beat,
The common workin' people have got to take the seat
In Washington, Washington.

And I'm gonna tell you, workers, 'fore you cash in your checks:
They say "America First," but they mean "America Next!"
In Washington, Washington.[128]

Guthrie's songs were played and performed for a far-reaching audience on the radio stations NBC and CBS, as well as the popular CBS shows *The Treasury Hour* and *We the People*. This exposure dealt a death blow to most of the members of Congress implemented in Rogge's investigation.

The 1944 election resulted in Hamilton Fish losing his seat as a congressman after representing New York's Twenty-Sixth District for twenty-four years. Voters cited his potential involvement with Nazi agent

Viereck and his noninterventionist platform as the reasons for his defeat. In the final months of World War II, FBI agents were sent to Europe to gather evidence by interrogating captured German officials who had worked with Nazi intelligence officers. Bernd Gisevius, a former Nazi intelligence officer, directed agents to George Duesterberg, the chief finance minister who approved and documented payments to all American-based Nazi agents. However, all payments were made under code names through German embassies or fake businesses, making them hard to trace to specific people directly. In September 1945, the United States Army restricted FBI agents assigned to the case to liaison capacity, which blocked them from any investigative authority.[129]

Rogge's efforts to secure indictments for the members of Congress who collaborated with the Nazis were officially halted in October 1946. President Harry Truman ordered his attorney general, Tom Clark, to remove Rogge from the Department of Justice.[130] Clark stated that Rogge was terminated for "sharing confidential reports, which were not for public disclosure."[131] The other reason for his dismissal, Clark cited, was "testimony concerning the methods used by Rogge and his team in Germany to persuade a German civilian to testify against Americans whom the Department of Justice under Rogge was attempting to convict."[132] Clark was referring to the interrogation of Heribert von Strempel, during which the team put him in solitary confinement, deprived him of food and aggressively cross-examined him for an entire day—while von Strempel suffered health issues from his confinement, which could have compromised the results. Von Strempel was the secretary of the German embassy in Washington, D.C. He drew suspicion due to his direct contact with Viereck. In the aftermath of Viereck's 1941 indictment for not registering as a foreign agent, von Strempel returned to Germany. During the questioning by Rogge's agents, von Strempel stated, "The embassy staff was instructed to have as little contact with American isolationists as possible to avoid rousing the public opinion and thus hampering the isolationist elements. My only contact with isolationists was when providing resources for Viereck."[133] No member of Congress who worked with Nazi agents was indicted or held legally accountable, but most, like Fish, were voted out of office.

CHAPTER 10

SPIES LURKING IN THE SHADOWS

According to a 1942 naval intelligence report, eighty of the United States' top defense-contracted plants employed at least ten individuals who were vocal about their pro-Nazi beliefs or were affiliated with a pro-fascist organization. The report elaborated that these individuals could attempt to help the Axis powers by slowing down production or gathering intelligence.[134] Cited in the report was defense contractor Textile Machine Works in Wyomissing, Pennsylvania (tasked with building machine gun parts), which employed twenty-three active German American Bund members. Plant inspector Paul Kullman and chief draftsman Joseph Held were personal friends with Bund leader Fritz Kuhn and Camp Siegfried manager Wilhelm Kunze. Furthering concerns, the plant owners, Theodore Thun and Henry Janssen, were vocal supporters of Hitler and had been known to travel back and forth to Germany.[135] The pro-Nazi influence within the plant's ranks made it a vulnerable target for Nazi espionage or sabotage. Textile Machine Works, a small defense plant, was limited in its impact on the war effort but represented an overall concern about the ability of potential Nazi agents to embed themselves into defense manufacturing. Unlike that of Wyomissing, the industrial strength of the New York City metro area would be a prize for any Nazi sabotage or intelligence gathering.

Brooklyn Navy Yard was the largest naval construction facility in the United States, repairing or building five thousand naval boats used in

Europe during World War II. Nazi agents focused on the navy yard as a top target for sabotage. Long Island's Nassau and Suffolk Counties were home to the Grumman, Republic, Sperry, Fairchild, Brewster, Ranger, Liberty and Columbia aviation plants. Fighter planes like the P-47 Thunderbolt, the Hellcat and Avenger bombers rolled off their assembly lines by the thousands—with cutting-edge bombsights and autopilot technology that Nazi Germany was eager to replicate. The Nazis created three major spy rings, which operated as individual cells that connected the East and West Coasts of the United States to multiple companies that third-party South American German expats owned. These spies infiltrated the communities of Long Island, Queens, Brooklyn and the Bronx, posing as housewives, engineers, students or United States Army soldiers—or even your neighbor next door. Despite the varied roles they played in their local communities, these spies had monetary motives and a passion for Nazi ideology in common. German Bund meetings and annual retreats such as Camp Siegfried became prime locations for Nazi officials to recruit the next wave of spies. During Siegfried's events, members spoke about "Der Tag," the day they would be called into service to help the Nazi Reich. Following the arrest of Fritz Kuhn and attempts to disband the Bund, members became fragmented but remained willing to demonstrate their loyalty to the Reich. Grumman and Republic Aviation employed over fifty thousand workers, providing opportunities for dozens of pro-Nazi American fascists to weave themselves into the defense contracting workforce.

THE RUMRICH SPY RING

The first of the three uncovered spy rings was known as the Rumrich ring—the first international spying case investigated by the FBI. The ring was estimated to consist of ten to fifteen agents, but only four were apprehended. Unlike the other two rings, the Rumrich ring did not rely on the German American Bund for its recruitment. The spies were recruited and worked across Long Island, New York City and the Panama Canal Zone. Many of the spies evaded the FBI by fleeing to Germany. Their objective was to cause damage to local military bases and shipping centers while gathering intelligence on Republic Aviation's new technologies. The FBI and the press named the ring after spy and, later, cooperating witness Guenther Rumrich.

Born in Chicago to Austrian-born parents, Rumrich moved to Hungary in his early adolescence. In 1929, he returned to the United States and joined the army. Within months of enlisting, he went AWOL but surrendered to authorities. He was reassigned to the army base in Fort Hamilton, Brooklyn, for the remainder of his term. In April 1933, he reenlisted and was assigned to the Panama Canal Zone. During his years stationed there, Rumrich befriended U.S. Army Private Erich Glaser. In 1936, Rumrich went AWOL again and was discharged from the army. He settled in the Bronx and got married. Shortly thereafter, it is speculated, he met a German agent who arranged payments of fifty dollars a month to him in return for providing details on troop activity he witnessed in the Panama Canal Zone.

When Erich Glaser was discharged from the army, he moved in with Rumrich to settle into civilian life. Faced with limited opportunities, Glaser reenlisted in the army at a higher rank and was assigned to Mitchel Field Army Air Corps base in Hempstead, Long Island. While Rumrich was helping Glaser study for his promotion to a higher rank, he noticed a set of signals in Glaser's notes.[136] According to witnesses, Glaser told Rumrich that the signals were for communication between airplanes and landing fields.[137] Rumrich copied the signals down and later shared them with Nazi agents. Rumrich attempted to get Glaser to participate actively in the spy network, but Glaser would limit his role to providing only enlisted army magazines and newsletters for his handlers.

The heads of the spy ring were German officers Erich Pfeiffer and Karl Schlueter, who were considered traveling agents in the Nazi intelligence service. Schlueter was a manager on the *Europa Ocean* liner, which came in and out of New York City ports daily. Hairdresser Johanna Hoffman collaborated with Schlueter on the liner. Schlueter recruited Hoffman to the ring, charming her and promising he'd take her to popular New York City cabarets during shore excursions. Through Schlueter's charm, Hoffman was persuaded to work as a courier, transporting intelligence gathered from agents to Germany. At one point, early on, Hoffman told Schlueter she wanted nothing more to do with him. Schlueter, in response, told her, "I am a stormtrooper leader, and I promise to make things bad for you."[138] Hoffman took this threat seriously because her father lived in Dresden and relied on a German state pension.

William Lonkowski, known by his code name, Agent Sex, rented an apartment with his wife in Hempstead. Lonkowski worked at a Seversky Aviation (later renamed Republic) subcontractor, but the circumstances of his recruitment into the ring remain unclear. His connections with floor manager Werner Gudenberg of Curtis Aircraft in Buffalo, New York, enabled him to obtain various blueprints for aircraft components, which he gave to Schlueter to smuggle out to Germany. Expanding his aircraft intelligence reach, Lonkowski would recruit Otto Voss of Floral Park, who worked as a mechanic for Seversky Aviation in Farmingdale. Voss received seventy-five dollars for delivering fuel tank plans, which he found in a garbage can on Seversky's production floor.[139] In October 1935, suspecting the ring was compromised, Lonkowski left the United States for Germany. Later, authorities would discover in his apartment dozens of photographs of an experimental U.S. bomber and notes on retractable landing gears.[140]

Schlueter provided all recruited members with an alphabet and hieroglyph-like images written on matchbooks. This was the unified code for transmitting messages between members. Later testimony against Schlueter revealed that the ring's plans evolved from gathering Seversky's aircraft-manufacturing secrets to obtaining plans from the navy yard for the new *Enterprise* aircraft carrier.[141] However, the ring's other, more obscure plans included perfecting the production of counterfeit White House stationery, forging President Roosevelt's signature and forging passports. Rumrich called the New York City Treasury Building's Passport Bureau, identified himself as Secretary of State Cordell Hull and requested that blank passport applications be sent to his hotel in Midtown Manhattan. The blanks were rerouted to a bar, with FBI agents watching, and after spy ring members received the applications, agents moved in and arrested Rumrich.[142] In custody, Rumrich confessed that if the passport applications had reached Europe, they would have been filled out with forged American names and addresses for spies who would branch out as far as Russia.[143] During further interrogation, Rumrich detailed an elaborate plot to kidnap Colonel Henry W.T. Elgin, the commanding officer of Fort Totten in Queens, and steal the coastal defense plans for the East Coast. Rumrich and his conspirators were going to lure the colonel to a Midtown hotel, where he was to be rendered unconscious with gas from a fountain pen.[144] The group abandoned this plan due to its potential for failure.

As the spies' identities became known, the Nazi agents started to scatter. Once his cover was exposed, Schlueter tried to flee the United States on the ocean liner *Columbus*, which was docked at Ellis Island. Following his arrest, Schlueter received a twenty-year prison sentence. Voss received a six-year sentence, Glaser a two-year sentence, Hoffman a four-year sentence and Rumrich, in exchange for his testimony against Schlueter, received a reduced sentence of two years. Most of the information gathered by the ring had little to no value to Germany. The only damaging information that came from the ring was the secret codes of the Air Service, which were stolen from Mitchel Field.

LUDWIG SPY RING

The Ludwig ring was the second spy operation discovered in New York. This ring was more structured but organized during a time when America was on the eve of war. Overseen by a Nazi officer, multiple members received training from Reich intelligence officials directly. The ring's participants were motivated not only by monetary incentives but also by ideological leanings. Kurt Ludwig, leader of the ring, was born in Ohio to first-generation German parents. In his twenties, he returned to Germany, and when the Nazis took control, he was promptly recruited for the war effort. Trained by the Nazi intelligence agency Abwehr, he was sent to Ridgewood, Queens, to build a spy network and shortwave radio stations. Within a brief period, Ludwig built one shortwave transmission station in Centerport (the first of two) and another in the cellar of a boardinghouse at 200–10 100th Avenue, Hollis, Queens. After establishing the radio stations, he made contact with Abwehr Captain Ulrich von der Osten. Osten would visit the boardinghouse under the assumed name Julio Lopez Lido and ask for a resident named Mr. Berger to gain access to the cellar.[145] Ludwig then embedded himself in Maspeth, Queens's German American Bund community. Members of the ring conveyed the intelligence they gathered via letters written in invisible ink to the transmission agent in Centerport.[146] Urgent intel would start with the code "write Marion Pon," meaning "notify Heinrich Himmler," head of the Gestapo.[147] The code names Grace, Betsy and Sarah represented the Grumman, Brewster aircraft factories and the Sperry aircraft instrument company.[148] The spies also implanted themselves in Republic Aviation and the smaller defense plants in the Nassau County Roosevelt Field area until early March 1941.

Lopez (Captain Osten) returned to New York after spending time in multiple locations of interest in the Caribbean and the Pacific. Most of the intelligence he acquired was from American military bases in Puerto Rico and on the Hawaiian island of Oahu, as well as from Naval Station Pearl Harbor. The intel he carried with him at the time of his arrival was from a naval military base in Puerto Rico. Lopez had dinner with Ludwig on the evening of March 18, 1941, and the two men were walking back to the hotel where they were staying when Lopez was struck and killed by a taxicab on Seventh Avenue in Times Square. Ludwig attempted to grab Lopez's briefcase, but Lopez's effects fell out. While investigating the accident, New York City police found the suitcase's contents. Inspection of the multiple notes in the suitcase revealed one that read:

> *This will be of interest mainly to our yellow allies—a strong concentration of troops. All Military establishments are prohibited for civilians. Fifty-seven officers of the FBI are said to be in Oahu alone. Questioning cannot be done openly.*

The message included photographs labeled "main fire control for guns" and "lookout posts." Additional notes included a list of defense garrisons throughout Puerto Rico, with annotations reading: "Seems to be still better to send somebody to Puerto Rico. Fellow passenger, lieutenant commander, been there in December."[149]

Following the discovery of the suitcase, the police turned it over to the New York City office of the FBI. The first arrest the FBI made based on the intel found in the suitcase of the deceased Lopez was that of Kurt Frederick Ludwig. Ludwig was arrested on August 3, 1941, in the remote town of Cle Elum, Washington, 216 miles from the Canadian border city of Vancouver. He was transferred to the Spokane County Jail after attempting to bribe a guard by offering $50,000 to assist in his escape. During interrogation, Ludwig refused to cooperate, despite the documents that implicated him.

The second most significant break for the FBI occurred on August 26, 1941, with the arrest of Queens resident Lucy Boehmler. Boehmler was eighteen years old at the time of her arrest and a recent graduate of Grover Cleveland High School. Before Lopez hired her as a secretary, she was a member of the German American Bund. The weekly rate promised to Boehmler for her services was twenty-five dollars. She accompanied Lopez on tours of airports, power plants, army bases and naval stations along the Atlantic Seaboard.[150] Lopez assigned her additional duties, such as charming soldiers with military information and making invisible ink from headache medication. Once in custody, Boehmler agreed to cooperate as a witness for the FBI, affirming that her allegiance was to the United States, not Germany. Her cooperation with the FBI led to the indictment and conviction of Ludwig and his seven other agents.

During her initial interrogation by the FBI, Boehmler disclosed that Ludwig kept multiple books detailing the identities, cargoes, origins and routes of American ships along the East Coast. In the back of one book, he listed the vessels that were destroyed, directly implicating him in the destruction of American ships.[151]

In later testimony, Boehmler implicated Helen Pauline Mayer as an active participant in the ring. Mayer, a twenty-five-year-old housewife from Ridgewood, Queens, was active in the German American Bund and a member of the German heritage group Turnverein. Her husband, Walter, was visiting Germany when war broke out between the Soviet Union and Germany, which left him unable to return to the United States; his connection to the spy ring was uncertain. Helen Mayer contacted and charmed Alfred Feil, a Grumman aviation worker in the Bethpage plant. On multiple occasions, Mayer attempted to get Feil to obstruct production at the plant. Feil, despite her requests, refused to participate. Mayer then told Feil he was a "very bad German." Feil underemphasized the plant's role in the war effort, stating the plant was "not so busy anyhow because of a lack of raw materials." Mayer was assigned to gather intelligence on the manufacturing details of the B-19 bomber before she was caught. Before getting caught, Ludwig had prepared Mayer for weeks to memorize the details she would gather before scheduling her return to Germany. While in Germany, she would share the intelligence gathered from memory with Nazi officials.

Early in September 1941, evidence and collaborating testimonies from Mayer and Boehmler led to the arrest of Fredrick Edward Schlosser, nineteen years old, and Hans Pagel, twenty years old, both machinists from Brooklyn. Schlosser and Pagel were members of the German American Bund, frequent guests at Camp Siegfried and, as adolescents, members of the German American Youth Movement (a Nazi-based youth program). Schlosser and Pagel were tasked with providing information on the cargo, origins and routes of the various ships listed in Ludwig's notebooks. Their recon included driving along the West Side Highway and walking around New York City harbors, taking notes of the boats docked there. One ship potentially linked to their intel was the Belgian SS *Ville de Liege*, which was sunk by a U-boat off the coast of Iceland'.[152]

The next group arrested was Karl Victor Mueller, a defense plant machinist with connections to the Centerport community; Rene Froehlich, a former U.S. Army private; Paul Borchardt, a former German army major; and Carl Herman Schroetter, a Miami-based boat captain. Mueller's job within the ring was to inquire about the production quotas of the defense plants in Queens and Long Island.

While Boehmler charmed soldiers and defense plant managers, Mueller assessed the Roosevelt and Mitchel Fields and the Grumman and Brewster factories, where he counted the planes and took notes on their accessories.[153] Mueller also cohosted meetings with other spy ring members in a Centerport restaurant to hand the intel off to a radio operator working at the Centerport shortwave transmission station.

Paul Borchardt was trained as a geographer for the German army and in gathering intel. Once in custody, Borchardt stated that in 1933, he was discharged from the German army for being a non-Aryan. He explained that he was "one of the 50,000 non-Aryans rounded up in Germany in 1938 and sent to Dachau concentration camp because a madman Jew murdered German diplomat von Rath in Paris." He described his stay in Dachau as brutal—until the German military police detained him in their headquarters instead. By 1940, he claimed, he'd obtained a refugee passport for the United States. On investigating Borchardt's immigration paperwork, law enforcement determined it was fraudulent. When asked about Borchardt's story, Boehmler stated, "He wanted to go back to his native land, and that was why he was doing this work." Carl Herman Schroetter was born in Germany but naturalized in 1930. Schroetter operated the charter boat *Echo of the Past* along the coast of Miami. Ludwig tasked Schroetter with providing information about military installations, plane deliveries to cargo ports and photos of military equipment in southern Florida.[154]

With all ring members identified and in custody, agents discovered additional documents detailing the intelligence gathered by the members and the intelligence Germany requested.

On the cold morning of February 3, 1942, Mathias Correa, United States attorney for the Southern District of New York, laid out the evidence before a jury. Judge Henry W. Goddard presided over the case. The press named the six defendants the Ludwig spy ring. Herman Schlosser's trial was held in the U.S. District Court for the Southern District of Florida. Boehmler and Pagel pleaded guilty before the trial in an effort for leniency. Since the group's activities were curtailed before the United States entered World War II, the defendants faced a maximum penalty of twenty years in prison instead of a death sentence.[155] Within a month of Correa making his case, the jury deliberated for two hours and forty minutes before deciding on a verdict. Once back in the courtroom, the jury's foreman, Maurice S. Gould, read from the verdict: "We find all six defendants guilty

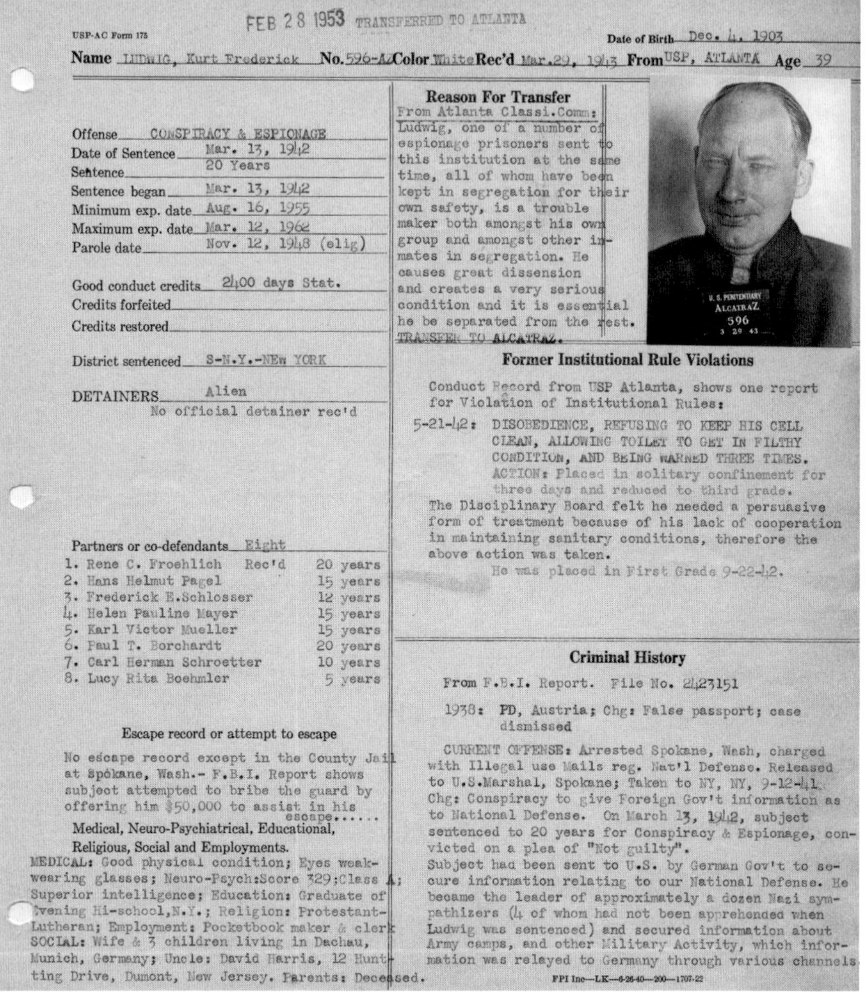

FEB 28 1953 TRANSFERRED TO ATLANTA

USP-AC Form 175

Date of Birth Dec. 4, 1903

Name LUDWIG, Kurt Frederick No. 596-AZ Color White Rec'd Mar. 29, 1943 From USP, ATLANTA Age 39

Offense CONSPIRACY & ESPIONAGE
Date of Sentence Mar. 13, 1942
Sentence 20 Years
Sentence began Mar. 13, 1942
Minimum exp. date Aug. 16, 1955
Maximum exp. date Mar. 12, 1962
Parole date Nov. 12, 1948 (elig)

Good conduct credits 2400 days Stat.
Credits forfeited
Credits restored

District sentenced S-N.Y.-NEW YORK

DETAINERS Alien
No official detainer rec'd

Partners or co-defendants Eight

1. Rene C. Froehlich Rec'd 20 years
2. Hans Helmut Pagel 15 years
3. Frederick E. Schlosser 12 years
4. Helen Pauline Mayer 15 years
5. Karl Victor Mueller 15 years
6. Paul T. Borchardt 20 years
7. Carl Herman Schroetter 10 years
8. Lucy Rita Boehmler 5 years

Escape record or attempt to escape

No escape record except in the County Jail at Spokane, Wash.- F.B.I. Report shows subject attempted to bribe the guard by offering him $50,000 to assist in his escape.....

Medical, Neuro-Psychiatrical, Educational, Religious, Social and Employments.

MEDICAL: Good physical condition; Eyes weak-wearing glasses; Neuro-Psych: Score 329; Class A; Superior intelligence; Education: Graduate of Evening Hi-school, N.Y.; Religion: Protestant-Lutheran; Employment: Pocketbook maker & clerk
SOCIAL: Wife & 3 children living in Dachau, Munich, Germany; Uncle: David Harris, 12 Hunting Drive, Dumont, New Jersey. Parents: Deceased.

Reason For Transfer

From Atlanta Classi. Comm: Ludwig, one of a number of espionage prisoners sent to this institution at the same time, all of whom have been kept in segregation for their own safety, is a trouble maker both amongst his own group and amongst other inmates in segregation. He causes great dissension and creates a very serious condition and it is essential he be separated from the rest. TRANSFER TO ALCATRAZ.

Former Institutional Rule Violations

Conduct Record from USP Atlanta, shows one report for Violation of Institutional Rules:

5-21-42: DISOBEDIENCE, REFUSING TO KEEP HIS CELL CLEAN, ALLOWING TOILET TO GET IN FILTHY CONDITION, AND BEING WARNED THREE TIMES.
ACTION: Placed in solitary confinement for three days and reduced to third grade.

The Disciplinary Board felt he needed a persuasive form of treatment because of his lack of cooperation in maintaining sanitary conditions, therefore the above action was taken.
He was placed in First Grade 9-22-42.

Criminal History

From F.B.I. Report. File No. 2423151

1938: PD, Austria; Chg: False passport; case dismissed

CURRENT OFFENSE: Arrested Spokane, Wash, charged with Illegal use Mails reg. Nat'l Defense. Released to U.S. Marshal, Spokane; Taken to NY, NY, 9-12-41. Chg: Conspiracy to give Foreign Gov't information as to National Defense. On March 13, 1942, subject sentenced to 20 years for Conspiracy & Espionage, convicted on a plea of "Not guilty".
Subject had been sent to U.S. by German Gov't to secure information relating to our National Defense. He became the leader of approximately a dozen Nazi sympathizers (4 of whom had not been apprehended when Ludwig was sentenced) and secured information about Army camps, and other Military Activity, which information was relayed to Germany through various channels.

FPI Inc—LK—6-26-40—200—1707-22

An Alcatraz warden's notebook containing an inmate floor card for Frederick Ludwig. Ludwig, convicted of espionage, was sentenced to twenty years and served his time in inmate segregation. *National Archives.*

as charged." In response to the guilty verdict, Helen Mayer cried in the courtroom, Borchardt stared blankly down at his hands, Ludwig drew back his lips, Schlosser swallowed hard and Froehlich and Mueller sat expressionless as they digested their fate.[156]

After the verdict was read, the defendants' attorney motioned for Judge Goddard to set the verdict aside. Goddard replied, "Motion is denied—the evidence fully justifies the verdict."[157] The judge sentenced Rene C. Froehlich to twenty years, Hans Helmut Pagel to fifteen years, Frederick

E. Schlosser to twelve years, Helen Pauline Mayer to fifteen years, Karl Victor Mueller to fifteen years, Paul T. Borchardt to twenty years and Lucy Rita Boehmler to ten years. Carl Herman Schroetter was sentenced to ten years in Florida's Southern District Court.

By 1946, the last member of the Ludwig ring had been caught attempting to enter the United States through Canada: Teodoro Erdmann Erich Lau, an Argentine citizen and official Nazi paymaster for members of the ring. Through his businesses, he distributed Nazi-provided funds to members of the spy ring. Lau's code name in the ring was Bill, as verified in the documents discovered on Von der Osten's suitcase. Additional documents discovered connected Lau to a payment of $2,000 to Ludwig from the Nazi intelligence agency.[158] Lau was sentenced to ten years.

As federal agents uncovered the Ludwig ring, the thirty-three-person Duquesne Nazi spy ring was also unraveling.

Duquesne Spy Ring

On Saturday morning, June 28, 1941, Everett Roeder of Merrick, Long Island, was relaxing after a long week at work.[159] But the tranquility of this June morning was short-lived. Black cars carrying FBI agents pulled onto the front lawn of 210 Smith Street and stormed through Roeder's front door with guns drawn. Roeder offered no resistance and was taken into custody. Neighbors in the quiet town looked on as the cuffed Roeder was escorted into a waiting car, and a team of agents entered the home to gather evidence.

Roeder had two sons and a daughter, whom neighbors described as quiet and never spoke to anyone.[160] Roeder was a top engineer at Sperry Gyroscope Company in Garden City. His projects included bombsights, long-range guns for planes and cutting-edge autopilot technology. Like dozens of other Long Island companies, Sperry Gyroscope was rapidly hiring thousands of workers, with little to no security clearances, to fill its short-staffed workforce.[161] The Sperry Gyroscope Company's projects were confidential and produced exclusively for the United States Department of Defense. America was on the cusp of war and prioritizing military production. The idle aviation plants of a decade prior, which had suffered during the Great Depression, were flooded with government contracts and money. Roeder, who lived and worked at the center of this technological field, was an ideal candidate for Frederick Joubert Duquesne's spy ring.

Duquesne, born in 1877 in South Africa, was a veteran of the Boer Wars. His hatred of England derived from his service in a Boer Commandos unit in 1898 and being held as a prisoner of war by the English. After his stint as a POW, Duquesne was employed by the Belgian government as an emissary in the Congo. While there, he was hired as an instructor for President Theodore Roosevelt on big-game hunting.[162] Shortly after his service in Congo, he was hired by the pre-Nazi German government as a spy. His first run-in with authorities in the United States was in 1916, when he was briefly arrested as a suspected German agent. Within a decade of his arrest and release, Duquesne opened an air transport business called Air Terminals Company. Shortly thereafter, he began an intimate relationship with anti-Semitic fanatic Evelyn Lewis. Duquesne and Lewis became acquainted with Else Weustenfeld, who was a secretary for the German consulate's lawyer, Hans Ritter. Weustenfeld would later connect them to the head of Nazi espionage operations, Major Nickolaus Ritter.

With his new contacts in the consulate, Duquesne built a spy ring of thirty-three agents who worked in New York City's largest ports and companies such as Westinghouse Electric, Bendix Aviation, Pan American Airways, Sperry Gyroscope Company, Carl Norden Corporation and Ford Motor Company. Money was deposited from Nazi Germany in accounts at multiple Central American–based banks and then at Chase National Bank. Duquesne, managing these funds, provided payment to the network of spies. Once intel was received, Duquesne collaborated and shared it with the Ludwig ring. Lewis helped him organize the intel and assisted with shortwave radio transmissions abroad.

In February 1940, German agents put Duquesne in contact with William Sebold to transport information he and his agents had gathered to German handlers. In 1939, Sebold was recruited by the Gestapo for espionage operations when visiting his mother in Mulheim, Germany. Sebold agreed to cooperate with German officials due to fear of reprisals against family members still living in Germany.[163] After expressing his willingness to work with the Nazis, he received brief training in coded messaging and microphotographs. After being assigned his first mission, Sebold went to the American embassy in Cologne, Germany, and notified the representatives that he was willing to work with the FBI when he returned to the United States. Using the alias Harry Sawyer, Sebold settled into New York City.

In later testimony to the FBI, Sebold outlined that the additional thirty agents in the spy ring, like those in the Ludwig ring, had ties to the German

William Sebold was questioned by FBI agents after he turned himself over to authorities and agreed to testify against members of the Duquesne Spy Ring. *FBI archives.*

American Bund or supported Nazi ideology. When Sebold arrived in the United States, he met Duquesne before delivering his instructions. During this first meeting, Duquesne inquired about Sebold's thoughts on the America First Committee and advised him to attend its rally at Madison Square Garden.[164] Duquesne then elaborated on how he donated $3,000 to the America First Committee from the initial spy ring budget allocated by Germany. As their conversation finished, Duquesne shared his fantasy of blowing up Franklin Roosevelt's Hyde Park church when the president was in attendance.

After the introductions, Sebold contacted Lily Stein. Stein was a trained Nazi spy from Vienna, Austria. She delivered microphotograph instructions to Sebold when he arrived in the United States. His first task was to pass along the microphotograph instructions he received from Germany to Roeder. The second person Sebold named in the ring was Richard Eichenlaub, who operated Little Casio Restaurant near Yorkville's German American Bund national headquarters. Eichenlaub's restaurant was the base and safe house for all intelligence planning for the network of spies. The network's additional safe house was a shack in the marsh near Marine Park in Brooklyn. This old fisherman's shack was also one of their multiple shortwave radio stations. Paul Scholz, who formerly worked at a bookstore spreading Nazi propaganda, was tasked with building and maintaining the Marine Park shortwave radio station.

Eleven of the thirty-three agents were employed in or around the New York ports or shipyards. Paul Fehse was born in Germany and trained in Hamburg to conduct espionage missions related explicitly to marine intelligence. Fehse's cover job was as a cook aboard boats coming and going from New York City harbors. While working this job, Fehse would have all the agents within the New York shipyards and ports report to him on their progress and receive instructions on the required intelligence.

Paul Bante was born in Germany and was an active member of the German American Bund. He was connected to the Duquesne ring and one of the spies in the Rumrich ring who evaded capture. Bante's role in the ring was to create discontent among shipyard unions, which evolved to gathering intel on ships en route to England along with Nazi agent Paul Fehse. Before being caught, Bante received a new mission: to deliver dynamite and detonation caps to other agents. The agent who gave these instructions to him was German-born Heinrich Stade. Stade was also the person who connected Sebold to the agents within the New York ports. Additional agents were assigned to monitor ocean liners that were being modified for military service as troop transports.

The SS *America* was a 723-foot ocean liner commissioned in 1939. Docked in New York Harbor, the ocean liner became a fixture for Nazi spy Erwin Stigler. Stigler was employed in the kitchen as a butcher until the U.S. Navy took over the ship. The navy fitted the vessel with antiaircraft guns and dozens of naval guns and renamed it USS *West Point*. When Stigler was dismissed from his cover job on the liner, Hartwig Kleiss was tasked with gathering blueprints and details of the guns mounted along the ship's bow. German-born mechanic Alfred Brokoff worked on the engines of many of the ocean liners that were converted to troop carriers. Brokoff provided the timetables, cargo and routes of English-bound ocean liners. Axel Wheeler-Hill, brother of James Wheeler-Hill and the official spokesperson for German Bund leader Fritz Kuhn, was a truck driver who rode routes along various New York City ports. Hill was tasked with providing timetables and cargo information from the port adjacent to the USS *West Point*. In addition to gathering intel, Hill built a shortwave radio station in his Bronx apartment to send messages directly to the Germans about the intelligence.

New York naval bases contracted shipbuilders, which had Nazi agents operating within their employment pools. German-born Leo Waalen built and designed small crafts for the navy. Waalen provided the FBI's industrial defense contact protocol for securing defense contracts to his Nazi handlers. Such protocols were designed to shield military secrets from espionage or sabotage. Following his success in delivering the industrial protocols, Waalen gathered sea charts of the Atlantic coastline defenses. Unlike those who shared intelligence via shortwave radio, couriers were assigned to provide physical materials directly to Germany. Adolf Walischewski and Erich Strunk were seamen who worked on ships with European destinations. Walischewski's and Strunk's duties were confined to dropping off Waalen's intel to various Nazi contacts stationed in ports across Europe. The rapid delivery of stolen timetables, routes and defense charts assisted with various Nazi U-boat targets. The other agents were employed in multiple public works companies. Gustav Wilhelm Kaercher was born in Germany and came to America in 1923. He was employed by the American Gas and Electric Company in New York City and was part of the team designing a new electric substation. During his downtime, Kaercher led various chapters of the German American Bund and participated in summer fundraisers at Camp Siegfried in Yaphank. Within the spy ring, Kaercher created a coded table and call letters for radio transmissions that the various station operators used for communication with Nazi agents. Carl Reuper was a German-born New Jersey resident who worked at Westinghouse Electric Company in Jersey City. Reuper was the founder of the German-American Alliance and a frequent visitor to Bund meetings and all the Bund's camps in the tristate area.

A handful of Duquesne's agents were embedded, like Roeder, within multiple aviation industries. Herman Lang of Glendale, Queens, assisted in drawing the blueprints for the original Norden bombsight. A strong supporter of Hitler and the Nazi cause, Lang became a willing participant in the ring. In June 1938, Lang traveled to Berlin and was offered up to $20,000 for all the blueprints and engineering specs for the bombsight. On meeting with German agents, he gave them a partial blueprint, and he received his first $1,500 installment by sharing copies of his blueprints with Nazi Gestapo leaders. At the time of his arrest, Lang had $3,500 in the bank, deposited from banks in Germany.

Unlike Lang, Lieutenant Takeo Ezima of the Japanese command collaborated directly with Roeder on what technical advancements their air force needed and which of Sperry's projects he desired.[165] The Japanese allies of Nazi Germany collaborated with specific members of the ring to further technological advancements in their aviation force. Roeder was one of the highest-paid spies in the network, grossing $22,000 in less than two years. Unable to get the specs for some aviation components, Nazi officials recruited Max Blank, a German-born librarian employed with the New York City Library System. Blank was tasked with obtaining information about self-sealing gasoline tanks and plane brake systems.

By June 29, 1941, the FBI had arrested twenty-nine of the thirty-three spies; eighteen of the arrests were made in New York City or Long Island. Despite having an informant within the ring for almost two years, the FBI decided to make the arrests because of a detailed plot to target the General Electric Company plant in Schenectady, New York, with incendiary bombs. Sebold tipped off the FBI about the plot, which provided enough time for FBI Agent William Friedeman to secure an adjoining room at the New York City hotel where assigned participants in the plot were scheduled to meet. During this meeting, the FBI listened to Duquesne explain to Sebold that they would construct a phosphorus-based bomb disguised as a Chiclet gum. The usage of the bomb would depend on chewing the gum thoroughly and folding it around an additional compound to cause an explosive reaction.[166] Once the agents were in custody, United States Attorney General Francis Biddle filed charges of conspiring to violate Section 32 of Title 50 of the United States Code, which makes it illegal to transmit unlawful information affecting national defense and to use the information to injure the United States' interests.[167] Additional charges were filed against the defendants for failing to register as foreign agents. Out of the thirty-three defendants, nineteen pleaded guilty, while fourteen pleaded not guilty and proceeded to trial.

Attorney Frank Walsh represented Duquesne and five other defendants as the lead legal counsel. Walsh argued that no law was violated because the United States was not at war with Germany or its allies.

> *We have no law that requires us to enforce the British blockade. We were not at war with Germany in 1936, when the conspiracy began, and we are not at war now. Nothing has been shown to indicate that anything transmitted by these defendants affected the United States. They may have affected Britain and others, but not this country. You must consider whether the administration's policies towards Britain bind us or whether we are enforcing a law.*[168]

Despite the legal arguments from the defense attorneys, on December 12, 1941, all fourteen were found guilty. On January 3, 1942, Brooklyn

All thirty-three convicted members of the Duquesne spy ring. *FBI archives.*

Federal Court Judge Mortimer Byers handed down the sentences of all the defendants, which ranged from 1 year to 18 years, totaling up to 310 years in prison. Herman Lang's lawyer, George Washington Herz, told the judge before sentencing, "My client had a weakness but has never deliberately given the German Government any information." In response, Judge Byers stated,

> *He* [Lang] *of all men knew the value of the Norden bombsights. He, of all men, knew to what use it might be by the powers of the Axis in waging war on civilization. I sentence Herman Lang to serve 18 years in prison on the second count and two years for the first count.*[169]

Duquesne was sentenced to eighteen years in prison on the second count and two years on the first count and ordered to pay a $2,000 fine. Carl Reuper, Paul Scholz, Franz Stigler and Axel Wheeler-Hill were sentenced to sixteen years on espionage charges and two years to be served concurrently for not registering as a foreign agent. Paul Fehse and Everett Roeder accepted plea deals and were sentenced to fifteen and sixteen years.

One of the additional themes that played out in the Duquesne ring and other rings was planned sabotage operations in or around New York City ports. In the early afternoon of February 9, 1942, the SS *Normandie* caught fire in New York Harbor at Pier 88. Like all the others docked in city harbors,

The USS *Lafayette*, formerly named SS *Normandie* prior to 1942, on its side in the Hudson River, Pier 88, February 22, 1942. *U.S. Navy Photograph 80-G-410243, National Archives and Records Administration.*

the luxury ocean liner was being converted to a troop transporter. A welding torch near flammable material likely started the fire, but within less than ten days of the fire, a Senate committee voted unanimously to investigate for potential sabotage. The investigation concluded that the fire was "directly attributed to carelessness and lack of supervision." The report elaborated that the fire was not the work of saboteurs, but "New York piers could potentially provide abundant opportunities for sabotage."[170] Coast Guard Lieutenant Earl Brooks of Valley Stream, Long Island, and Lieutenant Lester Scott of Brooklyn were blamed for the fire due to negligence. Navy Secretary Frank Knox took no disciplinary action against the guardsmen but considered appointing an administrator to each of the navy's districts in New York. A few years into the war, U.S. Army officials had a Nazi officer in custody who claimed he worked for Nazi intelligence chief Walter Wilhelm. Under Wilhelm's direction, the Nazi agent said, he gave orders to German American Bund members working on the SS *Normandie* to light the devastating fire.

CHAPTER 11

THE BENSON HOUSE

Hitler's rise to power fostered a hostile environment toward academia in Germany. Between anti-Semitism and the purging of potential leftists, the German population studying in various universities fell from an estimated one hundred thousand to forty thousand. These factors led Germany's most notable scientists to flee to less hostile countries. Albert Einstein was one of many academics who came to the United States. Once he established residency, he secured a job at Princeton University and rented a second home in Southold, Suffolk County, on Old Grove Road. Following a late-night conversation in his Southold home with quantum physicists Leo Szilard and Eugene Wigner about Germany's ability to create a uranium-based bomb, Einstein and his fellow scientists developed a shared fear. With Germany's few remaining scientists and the resources it had accumulated during its recent invasions, the potential for a Nazi-made mega-bomb could become a reality.

On August 2, 1939, from his Southold home, Einstein wrote a letter to President Roosevelt, stating that Germany could use "large quantities of new radium-like elements that would generate a nuclear chain reaction which could be constructed into a bomb, carried in a boat that can explode not just a port but an entire surrounding territory." Einstein went on to explain that Hitler's invasion of Czechoslovakia was a dire warning, as the country possessed uranium ore that could be mined, but "Belgian Congo would have the larger source to make such a bomb." The letter was a wake-up call for the administration to start militarizing and gathering as much intelligence as it could related to Nazi Germany's ability to build a uranium-based bomb. This much-needed intelligence, which confirmed the Nazis' desire to obtain large amounts of uranium, would be gathered a little over twenty-five miles west of Einstein's Southold home in Wading River.

Shortwave radio and telegram transmission stations connected the North Shores of Eastern Long Island, Nassau County, to the Bronx, sending a flow of industrial intelligence to Hamburg, Germany. On May 25, 1940, FBI Agent Morris Price established a shortwave radio station in Centerport with a cooperating witness, William G. Sebold, a former Gestapo agent, to tap into the flow of intelligence. Sebold was given $1,000 to create an additional shortwave transmission station and safehouse to entrap other German spies operating in the tristate area.[171] The station transmitted between two hundred and three hundred messages to the Gestapo over sixteen months, providing various agents with false information. From the intel gathered in Centerport, agents discovered that Nazi officials were monitoring the U.S. troops to determine the likelihood of an Allied occupation of Iceland and Greenland.[172] The intel gathered, and the witness testimony of William Sebold led to the arrest of thirty-three Nazi spies. This success motivated the FBI to seek opportunities to establish additional radio transmission stations.

Jorge Mosquera, an Argentinian businessman who had lived in Germany for twenty years, attempted to return to South America at the start of World War II. The Nazi government allowed him to leave but refused to release his assets and cash reserves. The only way Nazi officials would allow the release of his money was if he agreed to participate in intelligence gathering in North and South America. Mosquera had no loyalty to the Nazi ideology, and when he reached Uruguay, he defected to United States agents.

Before defecting, Mosquera had been given funds from Germany to establish a shortwave radio station on Long Island to transmit information from other Nazi agents he had contact with in the New York City area.[173] On November 18, 1941, Mosquera was brought to New York from Uruguay at the expense of the FBI; his cover story was that he was returning from a business trip. Working with Mosquera, FBI agent and radio specialist Richard Millen sought two properties that the Nazis would consider appropriate for safe houses. One of the properties had to be isolated, not draw suspicion and be compatible with high frequencies for transatlantic transmission. The other property needed to be a legitimate-looking business that would not attract attention and be accessible as a drop-off point. The first safe house in Wading River was referred to as the Benson House. The Benson House was situated in a dense pine forest, making it an ideal location to conceal a twenty-foot radio tower among the trees. The second safe house, an office rented in New York City at 1475 Broadway, room 1210, was a secret drop-off point for German agents, which operated as a front for a Uruguayan businessman. The FBI named the project Operation Bodyguard. The objective was to weave themselves into multiple Nazi intelligence rings and feed the Germans fake intel to deceive them.

With the safe houses established, the FBI's chain of contacts became a priority. Mosquera's contacts included Elmer Carlton, owner of the Remle-Carlton Shipping Company, which the local German Bund used to ship and receive goods from Nazi Germany. The Remle-Carlton's shipping operation to and from Germany was illegal due to ties to Nazi Germany. This contact was essential because it directly linked German Bund leader Fritz Kuhn and local Bund leaders to Nazi German markets and, indirectly, to Hjalmar Schacht, Hitler's finance minister.[174] Unfortunately, early in the counteroperation, Carlton got suspicious about his daily meetings with Mosquera and started to distance himself from domestic spy operations.

Hans Blum was a German army officer who attended espionage school in Hamburg and was another trusted contact of Mosquera's. His crucial role in the Nazi ring was to establish a chain of spies while operating a chemical shipping business called Remy and Company. Blum became a vital, unsuspected resource in achieving the FBI's intelligence goals.

FBI Agent Donworth Johnson had his family move into the Benson House using a cover story: he was suffering from tuberculosis and needed to self-isolate. The secret counter-operation diverted electrical usage from utility companies to two Buick engines, anchored in the basement, with modified mufflers to cover the sound and prevent attention. The first of the thirty-one messages sent in 1942 to Hamburg was on February 17. The FBI agent at Benson House sending the message went by the code ND-98. This code name belonged to double agent Mosquera, and agents were unsure if the Nazi intelligence service, the Abwehr, would make the connection.[175] To the agents' surprise, contact was made with Hamburg within a few minutes. Call letters were established for the Benson House (MHO) and the Hamburg station (NPD). The second message established frequencies and times. Five days later, Benson sent Germany a message that stated, "Have important contact with an engineer at the Republic Airplane Factory on Long Island and the Brooklyn Navy Yard, which employs 40,000 people. Can obtain detailed written material and information from these people. It is necessary to pay fifty to one hundred dollars for each contact."

The Benson station's follow-up message included the specifications of the Republic Aviation P-47 fighter plane, which federal agents had cleared. Additional messages included orders for B-17 bombers and specific motors that Grumman used in its concept fighter planes. In total, Hamburg sent twenty-four messages requesting specific intel related to military-industrial production, natural resource reserves and shipment of weapons and troops. Eight of these Nazi messages drew the most attention from the FBI:

Message 15, sent on March 14, 1942, requested information about aluminum production in the United States for January and February 1942. If available, aluminum production information should also be furnished for March and April 1942.

Message 32, sent on April 15, 1942, requested the informant to furnish additional information about experiments on the uranium isotope U-235. The Office of Scientific Research and Development in Washington, D.C., was conducting experiments on this item. The informant was also asked to provide details about ships departing from New York City.

Message 33, sent on April 20, 1942, requested that the informant furnish additional information relative to message no. 26, transmitted on March 24, 1942, which stated that the U.S. Army had been secretly experimenting with gliders for a long time and had just issued its first order for one thousand wood gliders, each to hold fifty persons.

Message 34, sent on April 20, 1942, requested that the informant provide details about incoming and outgoing ships in New York Harbor, including cargo, ship identity, arrival date and destination.

Messages 35 and 36, received on April 26, requested information about the Republic P-47 Thunderbolt, a type of airplane. The informant was asked to obtain information about whether this model was equipped with pressure equipment for stratospheric flights, the type of construction of the same and the details of its operation, including the exhaust gas turbo supercharger. The message also asked about the type of propeller used, the armament, the number of rounds per minute and the amount of ammunition carried. Message 36 requested that the informant furnish the shipping activities of the P-47.

Message 41, received on May 4, 1942, requested information on the whereabouts of the *Queen Mary* and *Queen Elizabeth* ships. (Both ships were used for troop transport and docked in New York Harbor.)[176]

Message 32, related to uranium, validated Einstein's dire warning to President Roosevelt three years earlier. This message was one of the few reasons the administration began the Manhattan Project. The $2 billion

FBI agent Richard Millen, who operated the Benson House's radio transmissions. *FBI archives.*

project (now valued at over $30 billion) was expedited within months after receiving the message from Germany. Additional radio messages fed the Germans false information about the number of troops shipped from Camp Upton to Europe.[177]

Discovered during the Benson House operations was the reliance on other transmission stations in selecting targets for Nazi submarine missions. Nazi *U-123*, under the command of Reinhardt Hardegen, navigated the coast of Long Island to the entrance of New York Harbor. While lurking off the coast, many of its targets were based on intelligence about the departures and arrivals of supplies en route to the European Theater of War. On January 14, 1942, sixty miles off the coast of Montauk Point, Suffolk County, the tanker ship *Norness*, carrying 90,444 gallons of oil, was struck by three torpedoes on its starboard side near its engine room. Within a day of the unsuspected attack, twenty miles off the coast of Quogue, Suffolk County, two torpedoes hit a second oil tanker, the *Cumbria*. Movements of troop carriers, such as RMS *Queen Mary* and *Queen Elizabeth*, docked in New York Harbor were requested by Hamburg. The deployment of soldiers onto these carriers was protected by false intel. The deployment of the 133,000 troops from these carriers would help pave the way for the success of the D-Day invasion.

CHAPTER 12

FIGHTING MISINFORMATION THROUGH PROPAGANDA

As the fighting heated up in Europe and the Pacific, the United States had to prepare for its inevitable entrance into the war. For years, the Nazis spent millions of dollars on propaganda that targeted a breakdown of American unification. Public consumption of false news and rumors became one of the biggest threats to any necessary mobilization effort. In the aftermath of the Japanese attack on Pearl Harbor, the United States was forced out of isolation and put at the center of a global war. The United States' success in the war depended on repairing the damage to government trust caused by foreign propaganda. Mobilization would have to extend into every aspect of American society. Fascist propaganda spun by Lawrence Dennis and George Eggleton's work in mainstream media outlets such as *Reader's Digest* reached over four million daily subscribers. However, the most concerning method of delivering propaganda was radio shows that broadcasted the voices of pro-Nazi zealots into living rooms throughout the country.

Racist ideology and false news, marketed as truth, spurred the rise of demagogue figures such as Father Charles Coughlin, who cultivated a radio audience that numbered in the millions. Fueling his exposure, Coughlin advertised and sold subscriptions to the weekly magazine *Social Justice*. The stories reported in *Social Justice* had headlines like "The Jewish Question," "Peacetime Draft New Step to Dictatorship" and "Jews Put Pressure on Willkie to Hit at Father Coughlin." Coughlin's programming and magazine inspired the group Christian Front and other branch-offs of similar movements that built alliances with the Bund. Coughlin's massive audience and media machine drew public admiration from Julius Streicher, the editor of the Nazi newspaper *Der Stürmer*. In one of his newspapers, Streicher referred to Coughlin as a "model fascist."

The Coughlin-driven Christian Front made headlines in early January 1940 when seventeen members attempted to overthrow the United States government. Leader John Cassidy recruited multiple enlisted National Guard soldiers from New York's 165th, who provided ammunition and automatic weapons intended for targeted attacks on Jewish media outlets and left-leaning members of Congress. Once the attacks began, the 165th guard unit was to intervene, forcing General George Van Horn Moseley into power and overthrowing the democratically elected President Franklin D. Roosevelt. According to FBI informant Denis Healy, Gerald Bishop, who was Austrian-born, had deep-rooted connections to the Bund and was suspected of being a paid Nazi foreign agent. Bishop and John Cassidy's vision for overthrowing the government was ingrained by the ideas expressed in Coughlin's newspapers and radio broadcasts. In documents seized from Cassidy's Brooklyn home, the planned coup was described as "armed self-defense against the spread of communism from the Roosevelt administration." In closing, the plotters' manifesto stated, "We pledge to defend Rev. Charles Coughlin and all his true soldiers of Christ with the last drop of our blood." Additional evidence from searches and witness testimony came to light during the Christian Front defendants' trial. It was revealed that four hundred New York City police officers were active members of the Christian Front. Chartered National Rifle Association clubs conducted the weapons training of these members and other members of the Christian Front. Decades later, Cassidy would not denounce Coughlin and would argue that his broadcasts were only anti-communist, proclaiming himself a patriot.

Given the domestic vulnerability of radio airwaves, promoting propaganda through nightly shows became the ideal method of eroding trust in governmental institutions. Multiple Nazi programs were broadcast from Germany to the United States coast to coast, masking themselves as news sources. One of the shows with a broad audience was *Radio Debunk*, hosted by Joe Scanlon (whose real name was Herbert John Burgman) and advertised as "the voice of all free America." Burgman's broadcasts were approved by Nazi chief propagandist Joseph Goebbels and targeted stories about American mobilization and support of the war effort. Fictional stories by Burgman claimed that the British had no rationing and were allegedly joyriding on rationed American tires and gasoline. One of Burgman's other claims was that Roosevelt and Henry Morgenthau never intended to redeem war bond stamps.[178] Burgman, originally from Minnesota, had a thick Midwestern accent, convincing many listeners that his broadcasts were coming from the United States, not Berlin.

The United States government established the Office of War Information (OWI) on June 13, 1942, to counter the influence of Germany and anti-government voices. The OWI aimed to expand Americans' understanding of global events related to the war and advertise the need for American mobilization efforts. The office hired mainstream writers and movie directors to strategically launch a media blitz featuring films, posters, radio programs and newsletters to promote American mobilization and unity. Renowned detective thriller writer Rex Stout was given a daily radio show called *Our Secret Weapon: The Truth*. Every evening, Stout reaffirmed in the show's opening,

> *Do you know what our secret weapon is, you Americans? It is simply the truth. It is not a secret in our country, but a big secret for people who live in Germany, Japan, and Italy. Our enemies do not possess this weapon; they dare not tell their people the truth. Instead, they lie, lie, and lie. Every week, this program will expose Axis lies.*

Stout would proceed to debunk the daily dose of Axis propaganda for the remainder of the show.

Guiding the direction of Stout's show and the media blitz, the War Rumor Project was a key component for the success of the information wars. To assess the Nazi propagandists' multimedia campaigns, agents were recruited in every town in America, big and small, to listen or engage with and document any rumor related to the war, government, society or mobilization. The War Rumor Project defined a rumor based on three characteristics: (1) It is offered as a fact, not an opinion; (2) it carries the implications of a private, reliable source of information that is not available to the general public; and (3) it has a specific rather than a vague reference or half-truth.[179]

Following the initial data collection in 1942, the rumors were categorized into six groups based on their intention, source and objective. The majority of the rumors came from or were employed by Nazi propagandists.

> *The categories of the rumors include Mouse Trap Rumors, designed to raise unjustified hope and cause relaxation of the war effort. Has the intended*

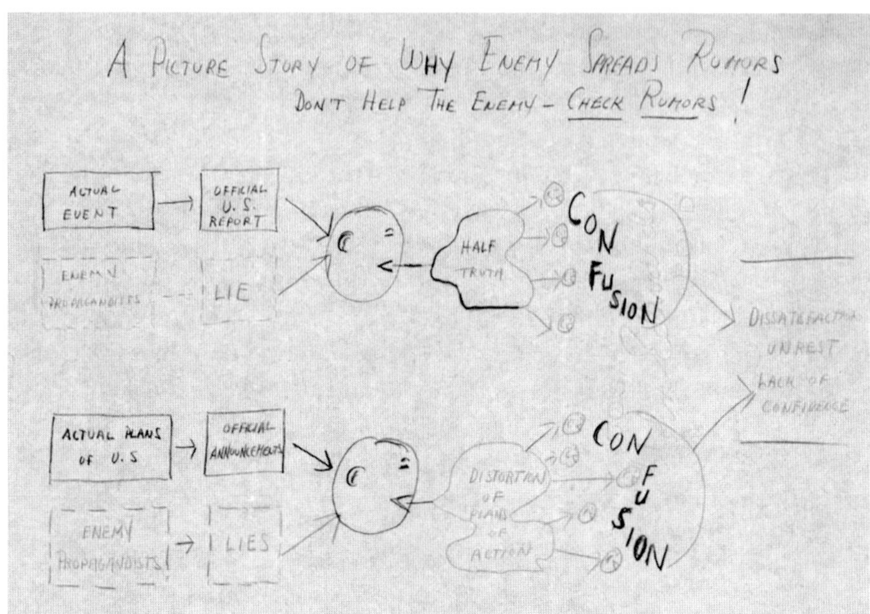
A Picture Story of Why Enemy Spreads Rumors
Don't Help The Enemy – Check Rumors!
Actual Event
Official U.S. Report
Enemy Propagandists
Lie
Half Truth
Confusion
Unrest
Actual Plans of U.S
Official Announcements
Enemy Propagandists
Lies
Distortion of Plans of Action
Confusion

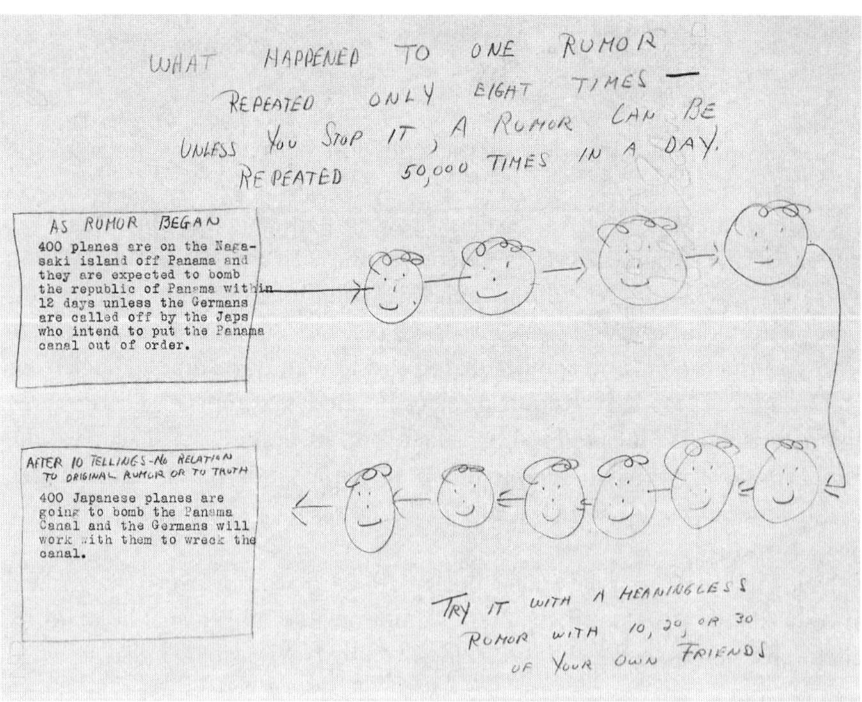
What happened to one rumor — repeated only eight times — unless you stop it, a rumor can be repeated 50,000 times in a day.
As Rumor Began
400 planes are on the Nagasaki island off Panama and they are expected to bomb the republic of Panama within 12 days unless the Germans are called off by the Japs who intend to put the Panama canal out of order.
After 10 tellings - No relation to original rumor or to truth
400 Japanese planes are going to bomb the Panama Canal and the Germans will work with them to wreck the canal.
Try it with a meaningless rumor with 10, 20, or 30 of your own friends

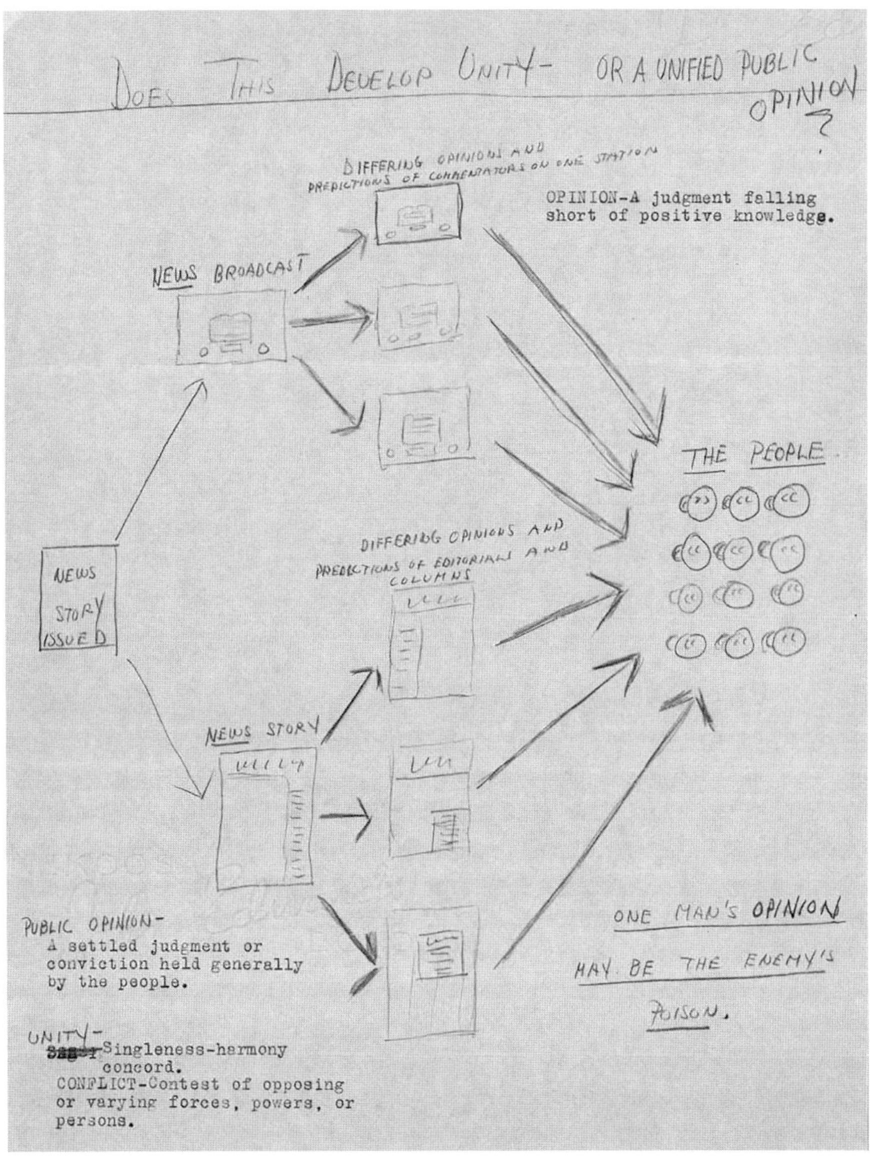

Opposite, top: A diagram from the World War II Rumor Project depicting how an enemy spreads half-truths and distorted truths, which confuses people who listen. *Library of Congress, World War II Rumor Project Collection.*

Opposite, bottom: A World War II Rumor Project diagram explaining what happens to one rumor when repeated nine times. *Library of Congress, World War II Rumor Project Collection.*

Above: A World War II Rumor Project diagram explaining how a rumor becomes public opinion. *Library of Congress, World War II Rumor Project Collection.*

consequence of slowing down production and mobilization. The Nazis used the Defeatist Rumor during the June 1940 invasion and surrender of France to the Germans. Not used in America, it started as a Mouse Trap Rumor. The Slanderous Rumor is targeted against institutions and leaders of a Nation. This rumor aims to erode a government's and its people's trust by questioning its physical and mental health, integrity, and effectiveness. The Strategic Rumor is directed to mislead people, the government, or the military. An example is creating a story of a potential military attack in one location to carry out a surprise attack at another. The Confused Rumor involves making two or more stories about the same subject, aiming to create confusion or erode faith in an institution. The Recurrent Rumor is used repeatedly to reaffirm a myth or story.[180]

Opposite and left: Based on information from the World War II Rumor Project, the Office of War Information created public awareness posters and pamphlets. This propaganda was used to debunk rumors and used the power of persuasion to gain support for the war effort. *Library of Congress, World War II Rumor Project Collection.*

The most common rumors of mobilization that plagued the local Army Air Corps base, Mitchel Field, targeted women recruits: "Those WAACs [Women's Auxiliary Army Corps] were hired to give the men in the U.S. Army women they wouldn't have to pay for. Each squad of men will get one woman." Another rumor circulated by Father Coughlin's followers in Brooklyn was: "The president ordered the establishment of the WAAC to get more control over the women of this country. He wants to see the home broken up, as it has been in atheistic Russia."[181]

Within New York City, rumors circulated about a depleted food supply. "There is going to be a tremendous food shortage. I know one farmer in Suffolk County who just plowed up forty acres of string beans because he couldn't get pickers."

Rumors about production spread by Christian Front members plagued communities surrounding aviation companies from New York City into Long Island. "Every second plane that comes off the line is defective and will go down in flames when it gets into battle." On the production line, rumors circulated that "the army is getting more and more control of production. First thing you know, we'll be under a U.S. Army dictatorship."

Once these rumors were collected, the War Rumor Project would reexamine the impact of the media blitz from the Office of War Information. Within a brief period, volunteers would report whether the rumor persisted. This method would evolve into additional multimedia outlets. Doubleday Publishing of Garden City, New York, released a line of books with titles such as *The Foe We Face*, by Pierre Huss, that highlighted the dangers posed by the Nazi Reich to American society. Publisher G.P. Putnam's Sons followed up with the books *The Voice of Destruction* by Herman Rauschning and *Silent Enemies* by Justina Hill, which detailed the threat of Nazism abroad and the Nazis' use of misinformation.

Multiple full-length movies influenced by the media blitz were produced to promote the war effort or boost morale during the war. The musical *This Is the Army* served as a morale booster, highlighting the current generation

Opposite and left: The Office of War Information used these public awareness posters to counter Nazi influence. *Library of Congress.*

Below: After the Office of War Information's public awareness campaign succeeded, local community groups designed awareness campaigns to gain support for the war effort. *Northridge University Library, Digital Collections.*

of soldiers learning from the prior generation that fought in World War I. Disney Studios retooled its studio layout so that 90 percent of its productions could be related to the war effort. Beloved characters such as Donald Duck depicted the Nazis as an immoral and oppressive government. After years of the Nazi propaganda machine sowing disunity, the United States mobilized all sources of its media to declare war on a shared enemy: fascism.

CHAPTER 13

LAST GASP OF NAZI INTELLIGENCE AND THE FORGOTTEN POW CAMPS

After Kuhn and other leaders were arrested, the Bund became fragmented. Despite all the aspiring American führers and their passion for a United States Reich, the increasingly bad reputation of the Bund based on its members' connections to the various spy rings caused a decline in membership. Many of its former members had joined the America First Committee by 1940. In the days that followed the bombing of Pearl Harbor, the Bund and the America First Committee officially disbanded. But the disbanding of these organizations did not reduce the potential threat to the United States from domestic radicalized pro-Nazi individuals. Throughout the duration of the war, the United States deployed forfeiture of Germany's assets in American banks and detained Bund members for internment.

The Roundup

The same week that America entered the war, the FBI expanded its investigations into German and Japanese businesses throughout the country. In New York City, hundreds of German and Japanese banks, shipping firms and other companies were forced to close, and their assets were frozen. Over $5 to $7 million worth of property was seized throughout the country within two weeks. One of the largest amounts frozen was $3 million held by the

New York City–based Union Banking Corporation. These funds belonged to German industrialist Fritz Thyssen, who was the financial backer of the early Nazi Party and Hitler. The financial manager of Thyssen's American assets was Cornelius Lievense, a Glen Head, Long Island resident. The funds Lievense oversaw were partially invested in the Harold Pennington firm of Garden City, Long Island. Lievense was not brought up on charges, and the funds were later restored because the assets had been deposited in the bank in the mid-1920s, and Thyssen had broken off his connection to the Nazis in 1939.

On January 14, 1942, the federal government implemented an enemy alien registration program. Enemy alien status became a concern due to intel coming out of Germany about the formation of a potential Nazi fifth column. Organized by leaders of the Gestapo and the SS Elite Guards, the fifth column would be utilized when the Nazis were facing inevitable defeat. The surviving leadership would activate a dormant resistance movement throughout Germany and the United States. The known connections of the Bund to various espionage and sabotage rings led government officials to believe that there could be multiple sleeper cells. President Franklin Roosevelt issued Executive Order 9066, which authorized the forced removal of all persons deemed a threat to national security. Throughout New York, all German, Italian and Japanese people fourteen years of age and older who were not American citizens were required to apply for a Certificate of Identification at the county office. If any of the persons cited in the law did not comply, they were declared enemy aliens and faced internment until the war was over. Once certified, they were to always carry their paperwork with them. This law later expanded to all Japanese citizens, regardless of their citizenship status. In New York City, an estimated 2,000 Japanese citizens were put under a curfew until it was determined they were not a threat to the federal government.[182] The number of people affected by this law was 5 million nationwide and 26,031 throughout New York City, Nassau and Suffolk Counties.

Within six months, the FBI targeted Bund-affiliated and other Nazi groups. Its first target was the German-American Vocational League, which Nazi Labor Front leader Robert Ley directly influenced. The group originated in Yorkville and operated in German communities throughout the city and Long Island. Its focus was organizing fundraisers for the Reich Winter Relief Fund and distributing Nazi propaganda sent by Germany. A total of 158 league members from Queens and Nassau Counties were declared enemy aliens and detained for internment. An additional 113

Bund members were arrested and declared enemy aliens by July 1942. Any Bund leader throughout the tristate area arrested was sent to Ellis Island. Bund unit leader and Lindenhurst native Carl Otto Bregler was convicted of conspiracy to counsel resistance against the Selective Service Act while in detention. He was sentenced to five years.

Johannes Kroeger, a forty-four-year-old German-born nationalist and former German soldier, was detained. Kroeger, unlike many of the arrested Germans, had been naturalized (in Mineola, in 1933), but further investigation revealed that he had connections to Nazi agents. His first job was as a property superintendent of the Robert Fulton Apartments in Hempstead. Kroeger became an active member of and had a local leadership role in the Friends of New Germany and, later, the German American Bund. He made contact with German agents in 1941, when he was in South America, attempting to get a passport to return to Germany. He then moved to Ketcham Avenue in Amityville and got a job with H.W. Leigh Bus Company. The bus company was tasked with transporting employees of Farmingdale Republic Aviation to work. Plant workers described Kroeger as "talking too much" and as very outgoing.[183] New York Director of the FBI P.E. Foxworth had agents arrest Kroeger on September 9, 1942, following Kroeger's attempt to obtain interviews with Roosevelt Field employees. Kroeger was charged with transmitting information about United States war shipping and aircraft production to Nazi Germany.[184] Once he was in custody, agents discovered various coded cables sent by him to German agents in Lisbon, Portugal. In a deal to avoid espionage charges that carried a thirty-year prison term or the death penalty, Kroeger agreed to plead guilty to violating the censorship law. On December 18, 1942, he was sentenced to eight years.

In Nassau County, the FBI conducted roundups of German nationalists who were not members of the Bund but still posed a potential threat to intelligence. The roundup brought in three suspects: Lisette Kapri, who was residing in Roosevelt Field Hotel with falsified paperwork that stated she was from Russia; Rolf Quarck, a German nationalist from Port Washington; and Ernest Nolte, a known German chemist who was working as an upholsterer in Garden City.[185] In Suffolk County, local law enforcement officials arrested Bruno Johannes Valianski of Central Islip under suspicion of Nazi collaboration and robbery. Valianski, a self-proclaimed Gestapo agent, was a recruiter for the local German American Cannon Fodder Armies of the Third Reich, a militarized Nazi group waiting to assist in the potential Nazi invasion of the United States.[186]

At the close of 1942, hundreds of businessmen with deep connections to Nazi-related corporations and Nazi sympathizers were initially sent to Camp Upton's alien internment camp or Ellis Island. Bund members were sent to the Fort Meade internment camp in Maryland or Fort Lincoln in North Dakota as the roundups intensified. In total, fifty-one Germans, eleven Italians and eighty-six Japanese-born New York residents were sent to Upton's internment camp. As the war drew to a close, the domestically detained "aliens" were sent to other camps to make room for German prisoners of war.

WOLF IN SHEEP'S CLOTHING

As the war evolved, a Nazi defeat became inevitable. Nazi leaders attempted to dress English-speaking Germans in U.S. Army uniforms and train them in popular American culture so they could embed themselves within multiple army units. This deception operation was code-named Operation Greif, and participants received much of their training from Americans returning to Germany under the Heim ins Reich policy. All chapters of the Bund and affiliated groups supported this campaign, promoting it in their camps, such as Siegfried. Former Bund members were ideal Nazi soldiers due to their accents and understanding of American pop culture.

The first test was during the Ardennes Counteroffensive. German soldiers were implanted in various ranks to create confusion and distrust within the army. Twenty-year-old U.S. Army Private Karl Max Wacker was one of the most embedded soldiers in the deception campaign. Wacker, a German American who returned to Germany and enlisted as a Nazi soldier, was ideal for Operation Greif. He fully defected to the United States during the war's final days. He renamed himself William Walker, a U.S. Army private suffering from amnesia and battle fatigue. Wacker claimed that after escaping a Nazi POW camp, he joined the fight in Berlin with the Soviets. When he was brought to the Camp Upton base hospital, army generals were in disbelief, as he had no documented military career. Federal agents would later learn that Wacker was a one-time resident of New York City and that his loyalties shifted toward the Germans when the FBI picked up his parents for being "dangerous aliens" due to their affiliations with the Bund. After his parents were deported, Wacker enrolled in a Nazi spy school and told the people closest to him that he would "do anything he could to help the

Germans win the war."[187] Once in Germany, he provided his handlers with information about the locations of airplane manufacturing plants across Long Island and troop convoy movements. Wacker was only sentenced to two years in prison.

Following the bust of Private Wacker, the army had concerns over another devastating leak from a Nazi spy or saboteur within military ranks. In December 1945, Sergeant Frank Hirt of the United States Army was arrested for conspiring to commit wartime espionage. A second-generation German, Frank Hirt split his residency between Berlin, Germany, and North Babylon, New York, on Arizona Avenue. While he was in Germany a decade before the start of the war, Hirt enlisted in the Hitler-Jugend (Nazi Youth) and moved through the ranks to join the Reinsfueheer's Storm Troopers. After moving up the ranks, he was recruited and trained by Nazi spy agent Karl Bauer. Returning to North Babylon in 1941, Hirt kept his rank and training closely guarded secrets. His neighbors noticed he had a large amount of money, which he claimed came from well-to-do grandparents.[188] Similar to dozens of others in North Babylon, Hirt enlisted in the army following the Japanese attacks on Pearl Harbor. While serving in the military, Hirt developed an interest in aircraft mechanics and pursued a career in the field. After obtaining the position, he was suspected of documenting American military plane technology and weaponry for Nazi agents in South America and Europe. During a military tribunal, Hirt admitted he was a Nazi-trained spy but claimed that when he came back to America, he distanced himself from the Nazis and enlisted in the army. He stated his loyalty was only to the United States during his service. In early March 1946, Hirt was acquitted of any wrongdoing. However, Karl Bauer received a thirty-year prison sentence in a separate trial. The attempts at espionage within the armed forces were unsuccessful, mainly due to a massive breakdown of morale within the German army.

POW Camps

As the war progressed, Nazi Germany's vision of a thousand-year Reich was shattered by advancing Allied troops. The myth of Aryan supremacy unraveled as 371,000 Nazi POWs were shipped to temporary detention camps in various parts of the United States. One of the first shipments of POWs to the United States was to Aliceville, Alabama. A local from Aliceville who witnessed the Germans getting off the trains said: "We did not know what kind of devils were going to get off the train. Guys with horns on their heads—the so-called Nazi supermen. But they were a bunch of whipped, haggard, washed-up, and beat-up kids. You kind of felt sorry for them."[189]

The POWs held on Long Island were between sixteen and fifty years old. When they arrived on Long Island, they were suffering from various physical and mental health problems. Being captured in long, bloody battles brought on not only the challenges of trauma but also malnutrition and different diseases. A total of eighty-nine POWs died while in detention at one of three camps: Camp Upton, Mason General Hospital and Mitchel Field. These soldiers were interred in section 2C of Long Island National Cemetery. As for the Nazis that were shipped stateside, U.S. military command stressed the humanitarian treatment of all detainees. Most camps were open dorms with access to local communities, and prisoners were assigned to work as farm laborers. The POWs were paid eighty cents a day, half the pay of a military private.

Camp Upton in Brookhaven held an estimated 1,500 POWs, and Mitchel Field in Hempstead held 300 throughout the war. The number of POWs held in Mason General in Deer Park for long-term detention—or throughout the war—remains unknown. The POWs held in Mason General Hospital were considered high-risk due to their mental state, high rank or suspected homosexual tendencies.[190] Mason General detainees were isolated from the other POWs, secured in locked rooms and given limited recreation time in monitored dayrooms.

Camp Upton was in the Pine Barrens region, approximately ten miles from Camp Siegfried. The camp, established during World War I, encompassed over nine thousand acres. It transitioned metropolitan inductees into army units and served as a waiting area until overseas assignments were issued. On September 1, 1944, army officials announced that the camp would suspend its operations as a reception area for army inductees. The camp was broken up into sections for a rehabilitation center, a detention center for AWOL soldiers and a holding area for people deemed a threat to the war effort.[191] What was not disclosed to the public was the section utilized for foreign POWs, which underwent a costly renovation.

With a high estimated number of POWs in dire physical and mental health, Upton opened a 3,500-bed hospital with non-restrictive dorms. The new construction was partially used to model the success of a democratic society, and it had every luxury possible. The facility had seventy-one barrack buildings, which included state-of-the-art medical technology, a dental wing,

Boxer Joe Lewis was the most famous guard at the Upton POW camp. *Courtesy of the Library of Congress. Photograph Catalog.*

a dayroom, a library, an indoor therapeutic swimming pool, a remedial gym, a bowling alley and a music studio. The prisoners' housing facilities were wooden structures with canvases stretched over them and a small coal stove. Five POWs were assigned to each structure. Camp officials modeled the fair

This page: The modified Camp Upton, pictured here, was meant to secure the growing number of POWs coming into America. *Courtesy of the Longwood Library, Bayles Local History Room and Photograph Archives.*

practices of capitalism, allowing the working POWs to use their earnings in the local canteen or store. The dorms were equipped with a school for the prisoners; there, they were taught academics in a reeducation program to combat the indoctrination of Nazism. Once they completed the reeducation program, detainees were sent back home to their countries of origin.

The camp's first group of foreign prisoners (not counting the domestic internment of the 148 New York residents born in Japan, Germany and Italy) consisted of the 45 crew members of the German ship *Odenwald*. This merchant ship was a blockade runner stocked with tires and other equipment for the German army. That same year, 3 Italians and 23 Germans from Colombia and Saint Lucia, who were suspected of participating in international espionage, were sent to Upton. A Swiss legation was put in charge of the German and Italian POWs, and they were to report back on whether they received fair treatment as prisoners and whether the United States was abiding by the Geneva Conventions. In a report, the Swiss legate stated that the camp made a much better impression on him than he had expected. After interviewing several detainees, he found that bland food was the main complaint.[192] Other complaints included the captain of *Odenwald* having to share a cabin with individuals of lower rank and that the visiting hours for domestic internees were too brief. Internee Hein Berthing stated that he and others were only allowed to see their wives once a week for fifteen minutes, and they demanded that this time be extended. Building on the visitation complaint, Hein further argued that the welfare of his family was in jeopardy due to his inability to earn a wage to send back to them.

In April 1945, the first shipment of five hundred German and Italian POWs arrived. Before their arrival, the domestic internees were shipped out to Camp Meade, Maryland. The prisoners were surprised at the amenities and resources available to them. A letter dated July 12, 1946, from a former Upton POW, Josef Kraft, who befriended a civilian worker at Upton named Pearsall, stated:

> *I often think about the good times at the Besches Mess in Camp Upton. In Germany, we have to do without quite a lot, which wasn't the case over there. Most often, I think of the good food and the smoking we had when I was together in the dining hall….Should you still work in the dining hall, please give my best regards to all who knew me, particularly the German women who worked there.*[193]

Anton-Günther-Schule

Staatliche Oberschule für Jungen

Annaberg i. Erzgeb.

Abgangs-Zeugnis.

Paul Emil Herbert S c h ö n h e r r

geboren zu Schlettau i. Erzgeb. am 13. Juli 1925

Sohn des Kaufmanns Herbert S c h ö n h e r r

wurde am 15. April 1936 in die Klasse VI(1) der Anton-Günther-Schule zu Annaberg i. Erzgeb., Staatliche Oberschule für Jungen, aufgenommen und verläßt die Anstalt am 15. Mai 1943 aus Klasse 8. Beim Abgang sind ihm folgende Zensuren erteilt worden:

Allgemeine Beurteilung:

Schönherr ist in den Leibesübungen einsatzbereit.Seine Leistungen in den Wissenschaften und Künsten entsprechen seinen Anlagen.und seinem Fleiß.

Fachzensuren:

Fach	Note	Fach	Note
Deutsch	2	Physik	3
Geschichte	2	Rechnen und Mathematik	4
Erdkunde	2	Englisch	4
Kunsterziehung	2	Latein	3
Musik	3	Religionslehre	–
Biologie	2	Französische Arbeitsgemeinschaft	–
Chemie	4		–
	–		–

Bemerkungen:

Dem Schüler wird auf Grund der nachgewiesenen Einberufung zum Wehrdienst gemäß Erlaß des Herrn Reichsministers für Wissenschaft, Erziehung und Volksbildung vom 8. September 1939 - E III a Nr.1947, W, RV (b) - die Reife zuerkannt.

Annaberg i. Erzgeb.,

am 15. Mai 1943

(Schulstempel)

Oberstudiendirektor

Bedeutung der Ziffern:
1 = sehr gut, 2 = gut, 3 = befriedigend, 4 = ausreichend, 5 = mangelhaft, 6 = ungenügend.

This paperwork about the ranks of Nazi soldiers was found on a POW being processed at Camp Upton. *Courtesy of the Longwood Library, Bayles Local History Room and Photograph Archives.*

ARMY SERVICE FORCES
Second Service Command
1234th SCU PW Camp
Camp Upton New York

31 March 1946

I certify that Prisoner of War S C H O E N H E R R , PAUL ISN 31G 12 000 was received at the 1234th SCU PW Camp, Camp Upton, N.Y. as a "Detained Prisoner of War". During the time he has been under our jurisdiction his work and behaviour has been very satisfactory or better. Although he was classified as "Detained" pursuant to instructions received from higher authority, his actions and attitude while here have been in direct contradiction to the teachings and doctrine of the Nazi party. His performance of duty and his attitude have been such as to win the approbation and respect of the American personnel of this camp and the personnel under whom he worked.

He has shown a great interest in the classes conducted by our Intellectual Diversion Section for the re-orientation of the German Prisoners of War to the "American Way" of living.

It is my firm conviction that, as a result of the classes in which he participated, and as a result of the close contact with the PW staff and other American personnel, he has acquired a favorable attitude toward "American ideology"; and as a civilian will be a decided asset to the United Nations in any re-orientation program we may undertake for Germany.

A. L. Haggart
A.L.HAGGART
Lt.Col CAC
Comdg.

A behavior recommendation report and personal reference for German POW Paul Schoenherr, who was held at Camp Upton in March 1946. *Courtesy of the Longwood Library, Bayles Local History Room and Photograph Archives.*

PRISONER OF WAR CAMP

CAMP UPTON, LONG ISLAND

This **certificate of achievement** is awarded to

Paul Schoenherr

who has succesfully completed a course in English conversation

for Prisoners of War conducted at CAMP UPTON, New York.

In witness thereof, the undersigned have hereunto set their names this

______ day of April 10. 1946.

Edwin L. Dooley
1st Lt., CMP Ass't Executive Officer

Wilhelm Fischer
PW Director of Studies

A. L. HAGGART
Lt. Col., CAC PW Camp Commander

The treatment and abundant resources shared with the German POWs displayed the failures of Nazism and the success of American democracy.

Following the influx of prisoners to the camp in 1945, POWs were put to work as truck drivers, and Albert Goll, the commander of the Sayville American Legion, took notice. In a formal complaint, Goll said the POWs were authorized by the federal government only to do farm work, as there was a shortage. Assigning POWs as truck drivers had never been authorized, as that was usually a job reserved for American veterans.[194]

Once this letter became public, locals started to criticize the treatment of POWs in the camp. Parents of soldiers or veterans in surrounding communities became enraged that the detainees were receiving better medical care, dental care and educational programs than they were. A local paper stated, "Mitchel Field and Camp Upton have coddled enemy prisoners at the expense of American wounded soldiers and even chastised them with a slap on the wrists."[195] These headlines led to rumors of riots from POWs demanding more beer with their dinner, which created more local outrage. This rumor about extra beer came when many Americans could not afford a beer with their dinner, as rationed food in the markets was still a reality. But the POWs' treatment by military officials was viewed as key

ARMY SERVICE FORCES
SECOND SERVICE COMMAND
1234th SCU PW CAMP
CAMP UPTON, NEW YORK

201 - Schoenherr, Paul 10 April 1946

C E R T I F I C A T E

To Whom It May Concern:

I certify that PW Paul SCHOENHERR, 31 G 12000, has been a member of the 1234th SCU PW Camp, Camp Upton, N. Y., since 20 November 1945. Throughout his stay at this camp he has been very cooperative, and has been an excellent worker. He gave active support to the intellectual diversion program at this camp, first as a student, and later as an instructor in English. He is favorably disposed toward American Ideology.

A. L. Haggart
A. L. HAGGART
Lt Col CAC
Commanding

Above and opposite: Paul Schoenherr's certificate of completion for a deradicalization program. This program taught POWs the American values of democracy and the English language. *Courtesy of the Longwood Library, Bayles Local History Room and Photograph Archives.*

to the deradicalization of Nazism, which had a cult-like hold over the typical German soldier. Demystifying Hitlerism as a failure to these soldiers would help in the overall goal of building a postwar Germany.

Fritz Kuhn Becomes a Stranger in Germany

In June 1943, Fritz Kuhn was paroled from Clinton Prison in Dannemora, New York, and under federal mandate, his citizenship status was revoked. While he was imprisoned, the federal government had started deportation proceedings against him. Despite multiple appeals to vacate the deportation order, Attorney General Tom Clark ruled that "Kuhn was and is an enemy alien dangerous to public peace and safety of the United States because he had adhered to the Government of Germany and the National Socialist principles."[196] In a press statement, the chairman of the state parole board, Frederick Moran, announced: "Deportation, of course, being impossible at present, the United States Attorney has assured us Kuhn will be taken from prison directly to an internment camp."

The internment camp Kuhn was sent to was located in Crystal City, Texas; he was later moved to Fort Stanton, New Mexico. While at Fort Stanton, Kuhn attempted to garner media attention by staging a hunger strike with twenty-five other detained Bund members over a lack of recreational facilities. After two weeks, Kuhn showed no signs of being famished, and camp officials stated that he had a secret food stash in the dorm.

By September 15, 1945, World War II had ended with an Allied victory, and the deportation of Fritz Kuhn and 715 other detainees was scheduled. Wearing khaki slacks and a button-down, holding two suitcases with all his remaining possessions, Kuhn boarded *Winchester Victory*, one of two ships departing to Germany, docked at Pier One in Manhattan. When he arrived in Germany, Kuhn was taken into custody by American intelligence officers and put in the 106th Regiment prisoner of war camp near Heidelberg until he was deemed not a threat to the Allied occupation of Germany. A spokesperson for the military command stated: "He [Kuhn] is one of the greatest security threats in the American zone [American-occupied Germany]. As long as there are occupation forces in Germany, he might gather henchmen and threaten our security."

After extensive investigations into a possible resurgence of Nazi power, Kuhn was released on April 25, 1946. He was deemed to have no influence, recognized as an unknown to the German population, freed and sent to Munich. But Kuhn's legal troubles were far from over. In the aftermath of the war, Germany was rebuilding its country and denazifying. All relics of the Nazi government were being removed, and individuals who contributed to the Third Reich were being tried and imprisoned, given sentences that ranged from life to probation. Within a little over a year of being free, Kuhn was arrested and charged with participating as a ward chief for the Nazi Party. While awaiting trial, Kuhn was held at the former Dachau concentration camp until February 1948, when he escaped. As German officials conducted a manhunt in the surrounding areas, the court tried him in absentia. He was finally caught in the summer of 1948 and sentenced to ten years, but his sentence was reduced on appeal to two years, time served. By 1951, the fifty-five-year-old Kuhn's health was failing, and on December 14, he died. His death was reported in the press by his lawyer, Otto Gritschneder, on February 2, 1953, over a year later. Gritschneder, in an interview, described Kuhn's last days as "far different from those of his strutting in the United States in the 1930s when Hitler's power was growing."[197] In his last days, Kuhn was poor, working as a chemist far from the public limelight he once craved.

CHAPTER 14

THE SHADOW OF CAMP SIEGFRIED

Camp Siegfried had an uncertain future and was in a financial downward spiral during the war. One of the many Bund development companies that held a lien on Siegfried filed a foreclosure notice for $9,200. The management company, German American Settlement League, argued in court that $7,800 had been paid. After receiving a discharge of foreclosure and satisfaction of the lien, the league attempted to denazify the community. Returning soldiers who fought in the European Theater brought home with them firsthand accounts of Nazi horrors. Following European demobilization, these stories were reaffirmed in the Nuremberg Trials, which were detailed in every newspaper and newsreel throughout the country, providing a vivid account of the Holocaust's atrocities. One of the most significant events of the trials was that the Nazi leader Herman Göring, whose name adorned the streets of Siegfried as the prophet to a cult, killed himself before he could be hanged as a common criminal. Siegfried's vision of an American Reich and the legacy of the Bund consigned itself to the great trash heap of history. The league petitioned the Township of Brookhaven to rename streets in the community from Adolf Hitler, Goebbels / Göring Streets to Herkimer, Linden and Steuben Streets, the names of local species of trees. A representative for the league told the town judge, Arthur Reich, that the residents "want to be good Americans and do not want those names. The original developers who started the community are now not associated with real-estate tracts." After the renaming, the development attempted to blend into the rural backdrop of Suffolk County.

In the decades following World War II, New York City's rural outskirts were transformed into thriving, unrecognizable communities. Spurred by the G.I. Bill, Nassau County's population increased from 672,765 in 1950 to 1,300,171 within ten years. In 1950, Suffolk County's population was 276,129; by 1960, it had risen to 666,784, which had a significant impact on the community surrounding Siegfried. Yaphank's population grew from 1,500 in 1950 to 2,852 in 1960 and 8,793 in 1970. This growth pushed the history of Siegfried's Nazi origins out of the collective memory of the surrounding hamlets. The growing obscurity of Siegfried's past helped the league revise its history and its role in Nazism.

As the community grew, Camp Siegfried was rebranded as Siegfried Park, with over fifty single-family homes. To live in the newly rebranded community, potential residents had to sign up as German American Settlement League members, similar to a residential co-op board. To become a member of the league, you had to be sponsored by a member over twenty-one years old and of German ethnicity. Once accepted into the league, members could rent the lot on which their home was constructed. According to the leasehold agreement, they owned the house, not the land, and were subject to the community's rules. The league could revoke their land lease if they did not fulfill their agreement. These rules restricted traditional mortgages for potential homebuyers but allowed sellers financing approved by the league.

Former Nazi street names were changed, but the Nazi Sig Rune Youth emblem that decorated the camp decades prior was reused or modified for the community house and letterhead. In an interview with the *Suffolk County News*, German American Settlement League President Bob Wheeler described the community as close-knit, stating, "Everybody is friends here, and there are no problems." When asked about the community's Nazi past, Wheeler said, "They're fine American people fond of their German background, a spirit which built the Settlement League. They were supportive of Hitler because he was strengthening their country. They were unaware of the atrocities going on there; then they felt duped when they heard the stories of Nazi crimes."[198] These symbols, the league's defense of the Nazi past and the community's leasehold agreements would face their first legal challenges in 2015.

In 1999, newlyweds Philip and Patricia Kneer were searching for an affordable house on Long Island. As it is today, in the late '90s, Long Island was facing a housing affordability crisis. A close family friend referred the Kneers to a home their recently deceased mother once owned. The price was $70,000 for a two-bedroom, one-bathroom house, which was a steal

„Unser Camp"

Unser Lager und die Fahnen
sind die neue Zeit,
der wir eine Gasse bahnen
in die Ewigkeit.

Dieses Büchlein soll künden von Camp Siegfried, dem Erholungsplatz des Amerikadeutschtums, soll erzählen von dem, was wir aus eigener Kraft unter Ueberwindung grösster Schwierigkeiten in der kurzen Zeitspanne von knapp drei Jahren aus einer verwahrlosten Farm auf Long Island gemacht haben.

Es ist ein eigen Ding um diese zwei Worte, „unser Camp", wie bei vielen, vielen tausend Volksgenossen die Sommersiedlung des Amerikadeutschen Siedlungsbundes kurzum heisst. Denn „unser Camp", das sind nicht die 65 Acker Land allein, aus denen Camp Siegfried besteht, noch die Gebäude darauf oder das in diesem Gelände investierte Kapital, nein „unser Camp" ist weit mehr als das.

„Unser Camp" ist das Erleben eines Feiertages in Licht und Sonne unter gleichgesinnten Menschen; ist das Erleben der wahren Volks- und Schicksalsgemeinschaft aller deutschen Menschen, in der einer für den anderen einsteht.

„Unser Camp" ist für Hunderte, ja Tausende, ein Stückchen Heimat geworden, ein Fleckchen Erde, von dem wir sagen können:

> All dies ist unser. Wir haben es mit unserer Hände Arbeit erworben. Nun halten wir es für uns und unsere Kinder. Hier, auf diesem unserer völkischen Gemeinschaft geweihtem Boden soll unser Werk Wurzeln fassen.

„Unser Camp" — das sind stille Abende am Lagerfeuer, aber auch flotte Marschmusik und flatternde Fahnen, der helle Klang kampffroher Lieder, beschauliche Stunden im Siedlerhäuschen und lustige Abende im geselligen Beisammensein.

„Unser Camp" in morgenfrischer Kühle und sommerlicher Glut, im Herbststurm und Wintersnacht, ist immer wieder schön, voller landschaftlicher Reize. Seine stillen Pfade am Seeufer entlang unter schattigen Bäumen, seine freundlichen Strassenzüge an den am Waldesrand liegenden Sommerhäusern vorbei, die Tische und Bänke unter den ehrwürdigen riesigen Tannen vor dem Wirtschaftsgebäude, der See selbst mit seinen schattigen Ufern, der grosse Sportplatz, die Hitler-Eiche und alles, was noch dazu gehört, sind uns ein immer neuer Anlass zur Freude am Errungenen, am eigenen Besitz.

Aber noch mehr ist „unser Camp"; uns und Tausenden ist es ein lebendiger Beweis dafür geworden, was erreicht werden kann, wenn die im Deutschtum schlummernden Kräfte in richtige Bahnen gelenkt und zielbewusste Arbeit geleistet wird. „Unser Camp" hat diese Kräfte geweckt, Camp Siegfried in seiner jetzigen Gestalt legt Zeugnis dieser zielbewussten Arbeit ab, darum ist uns „unser Camp" ein fortwährender Ansporn zu neuen Leistungen, zu neuer rastloser Arbeit im Interesse unseres Volkstums.

Möge darum auch dieses Büchlein bei den Freunden „unseres Camps" die Freude an dem bisher Geleisteten vertiefen und uns noch Fernstehende dazu bewegen, einmal hinauszukommen nach „unserem Camp".

Amerikadeutscher Siedlungsbund, Inc.
Ernst Müller, Präsident

The community bylaws of the German American Settlement include the Nazi Deutsches Jungvolk (German Youth) symbol, with a shovel added, on every page. The symbol also appears on all community letterhead. *Longwood Library, Bayles Local History Room and Photograph Archives.*

The sign in front of the German American Settlement. *Picture taken in 2014.*

compared to the surrounding areas. After viewing the home, the Kneers were interviewed by the German American Settlement League and questioned about their German lineage. Patricia was half Irish and German, but her mother was born in Berlin, and the board was impressed that she could speak fluent German, which she did during the interview. Once the Kneers were approved to join the league, they purchased the home and had their first child shortly thereafter.

In 2006, the Kneers had their second child, and they wanted to expand the home. After attempting to obtain a mortgage to add an extension to the home, the Kneers discovered that the house could not be mortgaged due to the leasehold agreement. The Kneer family then decided to put the home on the market, but came into conflict with community regulations that prevented them from advertising the sale of the home. Purchases and sales of homes in the community could only be made through German American Settlement League members' recommendations, not through real estate agents. When the Kneers asked the league to change the bylaws to allow them to advertise the home, representatives of the league told them, "It will sell—the summer is coming."[199] When they pushed further for the rules to be changed, board members argued that the older voting members did not want the change, unlike the younger members, and that the restrictions would be lifted in time. After multiple years of trying to sell the property, the Kneers retained a lawyer and officially filed a complaint with Long Island Housing Services. The lawsuit focused on three key areas: violations of the Civil Rights Act, the New York State Human Rights

Law, and the Suffolk County Human Rights Law. Violations of these laws occurred through the German American Settlement League's practice of restricting the sale or rental of dwellings based on race or national origin.

In 2016, New York Attorney General Eric Schneiderman announced a settlement between the league and the Kneer family. The Kneers were awarded $175,000, and the league would have to reappoint its leadership and submit regular compliance reports to the state. When a *New York Times* reporter asked Robert Kessler, settlement league president, about the community rules and the lawsuit, he replied: "Most people don't even know any of this happened here—it hardly comes up [referring to Camp Siegfried and the German Bund]. People in other parts of town look at us and think this is closed to non-Germans. This is not true. The Kneer family is just bitter they couldn't get the price they wanted for their home."[200]

NOTES

Nazi Invasion or an Invite to Come In

1. "Guardsman Foiled L.I. Spies: Youth Saw Landing, Played Dumb, Took Bribe, Then Sounded Alarm," *Newsday*, July 16, 1942.
2. Ibid.
3. Saboteurs Case 1942, CM 334178, Correspondence Part I, Record of the Office of the Judge Advocate General, Ernest Burger testimony, page 11, National Archives, Records of the Federal Bureau of Investigation.
4. Saboteurs Case 1942, CM 334178, Correspondence Part I, Record of the Office of the Judge Advocate General, FBI Agent Norval Wills of New York Office testimony, page 14, National Archives, Records of the Federal Bureau of Investigation.
5. Saboteurs Case 1942, CM 334178, Correspondence Part I, Record of the Office of the Judge Advocate General, FBI New York Office George Dasch testimony, page 79.
6. "Scope of Nazi Spy Plot Revealed: Men on Trial Vanguard of Sabotage Army—FBI," *Newsday*, July 10, 1942; "See Court-Martial for Spies: LI Coast Guard Silent on Part in Spy Case," *Newsday*, June 30, 1942.
7. Captain Keith Lyle, memo to General Cramer, Saboteurs Case 1942, CM 334178, Correspondence Part I, Record of the Office of the Judge Advocate General, page 2.
8. Dorothy Thompson, "Who Goes Nazi," *Harper's Magazine*, August 1941, https://harpers.org.

Breeding Ground for an American Reich

9. Christopher Verga, *The Ferguson Brothers Lynchings on Long Island: A Civil Rights Catalyst* (The History Press, 2022), 34.
10. H.W. Evans, "Alienism in the Democracy," *Kourier Magazine* 3, no. 8 (July 1927): 12–16.
11. "Klan Letter O.K.'s G.O.P. Candidates on State Ticket," *Brooklyn Daily Eagle*, November 4, 1924.
12. "Three Flaming Crosses Fired by the Ku Klux Klan to Frighten Negros in Long Island Towns," *New York Times*, February 13, 1923.
13. Andrew Pugliese, "Msgr. Quinn, a Candidate for Sainthood, Is Honored," Tablet, October 29, 2019, https://thetablet.org.
14. "Abducted Druggist Is Found in Hotel: Ernest Louis Unharmed by Alleged Klansmen Who Seized Him in Freeport," *New York Times*, August 28, 1924.
15. Lauren Young, *Hitler's Girl: The British Aristocracy and the Third Reich on the Eve of WWII* (Harper Press, 2022), 139.
16. "Nazis Broadcasting American Freedom, Station Debunk to Be Underground U.S. Radio," *New York Times*, March 31, 1942.
17. Sinclair Lewis, *It Can't Happen Here* (Signet Classics, 1935), 19.

Myth Building: The Foundation of the German American Bund

18. Arnie Bernstein, *Swastika Nation: Fritz Kuhn and the Rise and Fall of the German-American Bund* (St. Martin's Press, 2013), 16.
19. Philip Slomowitz, "Heinz Spanknoebel No Desperado, Only Ridiculous German," *Jewish Daily Bulletin*, October 29, 1933.
20. Gordon Bond, "Nazis Over Springfield," *GSL Magazine*, March 2013, 4.
21. Otto Tolischus, "Reich Propaganda Abroad Is Denied," *New York Times*, December 10, 1933.
22. "The Song That Nazis Sing as They March in Germany," *New York Times*, March 26, 1933.
23. "Paterson Bans Nazi Film. Showing of Horst Wessel Abandoned After Police Conference," *New York Times*, September 24, 1935.
24. "Nazis' Hand Seen in Activities Here: Dissenting Officers of Local German Group Stir Ire of Agents," *New York Times*, September 24, 1933.
25. "Nazi Tried to Seize a Newspaper Here: Spanknoebel Showed Document of Authority in Office of the Staats-Zeitung," *New York Times*, January 9, 1943.
26. "Nazis Bar Staats-Zeitung: Edict Against Newspaper Here Gives No Reason for Ban," *New York Times*, January 12, 1939.
27. "E.A.H., Attacks Friends of New Germany Editorial," *Brooklyn Daily Eagle*, September 18, 1935.
28. "Foreign News: Fomenter Ousted," *Time*, November 6, 1933, https://time.com.
29. "Nazi Agent Called Home to Explain, Spanknoebel Reported at Sea Under Orders from Berlin to Halt Activities Here," *New York Times*, October 27, 1933.

30. "Nazi Letters Link Consuls and Clubs: Officials Helped Get Members for Friends of Germany, House Inquiry Shows," *New York Times*, June 7, 1934.
31. "Foreign News: Fomenter Ousted."
32. "Nazi Activity Here Limited by Hitler: German Nationals Living in This Country Are Ordered to Avoid Political Affiliations," *New York Times*, December 25, 1935.
33. Jerry Voorhis Papers, Nazi Activities investigation, 1940, Claremont College Special Collections, Honnold/Mudd Library, Box 132, page 490.
34. Ibid., "Bund Members Join National Rifle Association," page 485.

Inside Siegfried

35. Verne Gay, "When Nazis Came to Yaphank: 'Camp Siegfried' Play Explores Dark Chapter in Long Island History," *Newsday*, November 17, 2022, https://www.newsday.com.
36. John Edgar Hoover, Federal Bureau of Investigation Memo Bund Principals, March 9, 1939, Subject Fritz Kuhn, FBI vault file 09085574-00, section 1, Fritz Kuhn, part 1, page 85.
37. Jerry Voorhis Papers, Nazi Activities investigation, 1940, Claremont College Special Collections, Honnold/Mudd Library, Box 132, "The Purpose of the Youth Group," page 467.
38. George Dewan, *Long Island: Our Story* (Newsday, 1998), 238.
39. Frederick Barkley, "Bund Youth Unit Denounced by Girl for Immorality," *New York Times*, August 19, 1939.
40. Jerry Voorhis Papers, Nazi Activities investigation, 1940, Claremont College Special Collections, Honnold/Mudd Library, Box 132, "New Detailed Instructions for Functions and Activities of Storm Troopers," page 494.

Resistance Against the American Nazis

41. "Kuhn Admits Aims Are Same as Nazis," *New York Times*, June 24, 1938.
42. Thomas Dewey, Non-sectarian Anti-Nazi League speech, November 11, 1938, Thomas Dewey Papers, University of Rochester.
43. "Dollar Bill Makes You Member of Order of '76," *Jewish Daily Bulletin*, December 10, 1933.
44. Daley Jason, "The Screenwriting Mystic Who Wanted to be the American Führer," *Smithsonian Magazine*, October 3, 2018, https://www.smithsonianmag.com/history/meet-screenwriting-mystic-who-wanted-be-american-fuhrer-180970449.
45. Fiorello LaGuardia Papers, Anti-Nazi Letters, Western Union Telegram from United Steel and Metal Workers to Mayor LaGuardia, May 9, 1934.
46. "Reds Rip Flag off Bremen, Throw It into Hudson River: 2,000 Battle the Police," *New York Times*, July 27, 1935.

47. "Breman Rioters Cheered by 20,000: Anti-Nazi Mass Meeting in the Garden Also Demands U.S. Shun Berlin Olympics," *New York Times*, August 9, 1935.
48. "Catholic Boycott on Olympics Urged," *New York Times*, July 31, 1935.
49. Associated Press, "YMCA Leaders Against Boycott," *New York Times*, October 24, 1935.
50. Edward Shapiro, "The World Labor Athletic Carnival of 1936: An American Anti-Nazi Protest," *American Jewish History* 74, no. 3 (March 1985): 255–73.
51. "Group to Boycott Schmeling Fight," *New York Times*, January 9, 1937.
52. Ibid.
53. "Untermyer Explains Schmeling Boycott: Anti-Nazis Object to Money Going to Germany, Appeal Sent to Boxing Board," *New York Times*, January 14, 1937.
54. "Nazis War Foreign Jews Against Demonstrations," *Nassau Daily Review*, November 11, 1938.
55. Jerry Voorhis Papers, Nazi Activities investigation, 1940, Claremont College Special Collections, Honnold/Mudd Library, Box 132, page 494.
56. "Foes of Nazis Will Seek Permits Unless U.S. Curbs Strong Arm Tactics," *New York Times*, April 24, 1938.
57. Ibid.
58. John Metcalfe, "Secrets of Nazi Army in the USA," *Chicago Daily Times*, September 9, 1937.
59. John Metcalfe, "I Am a U.S. Nazi Storm Trooper," *Chicago Sunday Times*, September 12, 1937.
60. "Anti-Jewish Tide Linked to Rackets: Metcalfe Says Most Propaganda Is Put Out by Groups Exploiting the Public," *New Times*, November 20, 1938.
61. "Defense of Bund Sent to Congress: Fritz Kuhn Denies Ties to Nazi Government in Long Notarized Statement," *New York Times*, October 15, 1938.
62. Gustave Neuss Jr., interview, Longwood Central School District, German American Bund and Yaphank, November 2, 2002, https://sites.google.com/longwoodcsd.org/longwoodjourney/hamlets/yaphank/the-gus-neuss-archives-of-articles-related-to-the-bund-at-yaphank/judge-neuss-letter-to-the-editor-of-the-island-news.
63. "Sale of Camp Siegfried in Yaphank to Negro Inhabitants Is Threatened," *Mid-Island Mail*, Medford, July 28, 1937.
64. "Few Nazis Registered Thus Far at Yaphank," *Mid-Island Mail*, Medford Station, October 13, 1937.
65. "Camp Siegfried Group Held for the Grand Jury," *Mid-Island Mail*, Medford Station, May 18, 1938.
66. "Story of Nazi Threats Holds 5 in High Bail," *New York Daily News*, May 8, 1938.
67. "Nazi Bund's Parade Barred: Lindenhurst Police Chief Bans Permit," *Nassau Daily Review Star*, May 10, 1938.
68. "Bund Denies Oath in Trial of Nazis," *Nassau Daily Review Star*, July 7, 1938.
69. Ibid.

70. "Bund Aid Says U.S. Will Salute in Nazi Fashion," *Herald Tribune*, July 8, 1938.
71. Ibid.
72. "Yaphank's Nazis Resent Bombing; Camp Siegfried Visitors Showered with Leaflets on Americanism Dropped from Airplane," *Nassau Daily Review Star*, July 18, 1938.
73. Ibid.
74. "Suffolk Acts to Oust Nazis from County," *Nassau Daily Review Star*, July 26, 1938.
75. "Camp Siegfried Convictions Reversed," *Mid-Island Mail*, November 9, 1938.
76. "Storm Troop Regalia at Bund Rally Banned," *Nassau Daily Review Star*, November 12, 1938.

Battle for Madison Square Garden

77. "Mayor to Permit Big Bund Meeting, Says Free Speech in This City Is Not the Kind Prevailing in Reich Under Hitler," *New York Times*, February 18, 1939.
78. Jerry Voorhis Papers, Nazi Activities investigation, 1940, Claremont College Special Collections, Honnold/Mudd Library, Box 132, "The Bund's Attitude Toward the American Form of Government," page 522.
79. "Bund Foes Protest Policing of Rally," *New York Times*, February 22, 1939.
80. Marc Kantrowitz, "Nazi Rally in NYC Proves Beginning of the End for German American Bund," *Massachusetts Lawyers Weekly*, April 19, 2024.
81. "Legislators Spurn Reds: Republicans Reject Support for Anti-Nazi Uniform Bill," *New York Times*, May 10, 1939.

Fall of Kuhn and the Bund

82. "Kuhn Is Arrested on Charges Theft of Bund's Funds," *Patchogue Advance*, May 26, 1939.
83. John Edgar Hoover, Federal Bureau of Investigation Memo to Edward Allen Tamm, Subject Fritz Kuhn, May 8, 1939, FBI vault file 09085574-00, section 5, Fritz Kuhn, part 6, page 22.
84. "Jury to Receive Kuhn Case Today," *Mid-Island Mail*, November 29, 1939.
85. "Kuhn Found Guilty on All Five Counts: He Faces 30 Years," *New York Times*, November 30, 1939.
86. "Kuhn Is Sentenced to 2½ to 5 Years as a Common Thief," *New York Times*, December 6, 1939.
87. "Kuhn Aides Raise Fund for Appeal," *Nassau Daily Review Star*, December 1, 1939.
88. "Deny New Site for Siegfried," *County Review*, June 20, 1940.

America's Next Führer

89. FBI report: Subject, Edward James Smythe and German American Bund, File number 62-54144, Series 1.1, Office Memorandum, to Director from Mr. D.M. Ladd, April 18, 1938, page 22.
90. Ibid.
91. "Fugitive Arrested as an Aide to Axis," *New York Times*, November 1, 1942.
92. Fiorello LaGuardia Papers, New York City Police Records of Sgt. Solomon, 19th Precinct, American Destiny Party Meeting Reports, July 2, 1940, page 249.
93. Knute Berger, "The Strange Case of the Northwest's Native American Nazi," PBS, December 15, 2016, https://www.cascadepbs.org.
94. Fiorello LaGuardia Papers, New York City Police Records of Lt. Mohramann, 23rd Precinct, American Destiny Party Meeting Reports, July 26, 1940, page 252.
95. Tom O'Connor, "Edward James Smyth Tells All Between Drinks and a $2 Bite; Tinhorn Fascist Is 'Going to Get Coughlin If It's the Last Thing I Do,'" *PM Daily*, March 23, 1943.
96. "Conspiracy Charge Ascribed to Gossip," *New York Times*, May 7, 1944.

Nazi Propaganda Machine: "Getting the Bang for Your Buck"

97. William Donovan and Edgar Mowrer, "Germans Said to Spend Vast Sums Abroad to Pave Way for Conquest: Donovan Writes $200,000,000 Is the Annual Outlay for Organization and Propaganda—Nazi Movement Seen as a Conspiracy," *New York Times*, August 23, 1940.
98. Ibid.
99. Drew Pearson, "Washington Merry-Go-Round: Rogge Report Reveals How Intelligent Americans Were Taken In to Such an Extent That They Spread Nazi Propaganda to Fool Other Americans," Bell Syndicate INC, John Wheeler Press, October 25, 1946.
100. Ibid.
101. Ibid.
102. Ibid.
103. Drew Pearson, "The Washington Merry-Go-Round: Nazi Diplomat Tells How U.S. Congressman Were Subsidized: Lundeen, Fish Day Used by German Propaganda Machine," Bell Syndicate INC, John Wheeler Press, July 11, 1946.
104. Ibid.
105. FBI report: Subject O.J. Rogge, File number 62-54144, Series 1.1, Office Memorandum, to Director from Mr. D.M. Ladd, January 1, 1947, page 6.
106. Ibid., 5.
107. Ibid., 5.
108. "Nazi Data Link Republican to 1940 Propaganda Drive, a Congressman Tried to Get Convention to Back Isolationism, Records State—Hamilton Fish Denies German Aid," *New York Times*, May 27, 1956.

109. Ibid.
110. Ibid.
111. "Fish Endorses Zionists: Wants Jerusalem to Be Seat of League of Nations," *New York Times*, March 16, 1923.
112. "U.S. At War: Two Out, One to Go," *Time*, May 11, 1942.
113. Pearson, "Nazi Diplomat Tells."
114. "Nye Hits FDR's Foreign Policy in Freeport Talk," *Newsday*, April 3, 1941.
115. Bradley Hart, *Hitler's American Friends: The Third Reich's Supporters in the United States* (St. Martin's Press, 2018), 177.
116. "Isolationists to Survey Movies for Propaganda," *Newsday*, June 6, 1941.
117. Ibid.
118. "Hill Links Fish with Viereck Acts: Convicted Secretary Reverses Testimony in Telling of His Introduction to Nazi Agent," *New York Times*, February 20, 1942.
119. "Anti-Semitic Propaganda Carried in Franked Envelopes of Congressman Fish," *Jewish Telegraph: Daily News Bulletin*, August 28, 1941.
120. "Fish's Aide Indicted as Perjurer: Franked Mail Involved in Counts," *New York Times*, October 25, 1941.
121. Ibid.
122. "Say Hill Ordered Mail Bags Moved, Three House Post Office Aides Tell Court There Was a Rush Pick Up After Subpoena," *New York Times*, January 13, 1942.
123. "Not Fish, but Foul," *Time*, January 26, 1942, https://time.com.
124. "Hill Links Fish."
125. Otto Schuler, letter to Thomas Dewey, June 16, 1942, Thomas Dewey Papers, University of Rochester.
126. Conversation between Thomas Dewey and Hamilton Fish, May 22, 1942, Thomas Dewey Papers, University of Rochester.
127. Gallup Organization, September 4–9, 1941, based on 1,500 personal interviews. Sample: National adult. The sample size is approximate. USGALLUP.41-248.QT11.
128. Woody Guthrie, "Mister Charles Lindbergh," Woody Guthrie Archives, Tulsa, Oklahoma, https://woodyguthrie.org.
129. John O'Donnell, "Capitol Stuff," *Times Herald*, April 9, 1947.
130. Ibid.
131. Associated Press, "Clark Outs Rogge for Speech Linking Americans with Nazis: Clark Dismisses Rogge for Speech," *New York Times*, October 26, 1946.
132. O'Donnell, "Capitol Stuff."
133. OSS memo: Subject Heribert von Strempel: SSU: CIA: Nazi War Crimes and Japanese Imperial Government Records Interagency Working Group, January 23, 1946, https://www.cia.gov/readingroom/docs/STREMPEL,%20HERBERT%20(VON)_0015.pdf.

Spies Lurking in the Shadows

134. J.B.W. Walker, Director of Naval Operations, "German Intelligence Activities in the United States and Counter Measures 1941," Navy Department Office of Chief of Naval Operations, January 24, 1942, Serial Number 0138716, page 3.
135. Ibid.
136. "Spy Says Agents Altered His Story: His Denial of Aim to Betray United States," *New York Times*, October 25, 1938.
137. Ibid.
138. "Hairdresser Tells of Threats by Spy," *New York Times*, November 11, 1938.
139. "Army & Navy: Spy Business," *Time*, November 14, 1938.
140. "Beautiful Brunette Tells of Nazi Spying in America," *Daily News*, October 27, 1938.
141. "Nazi Spy, Accused in Trial of Ring Here, Nabbed by FBI," *Nassau Daily Review-Star*, January 15, 1940.
142. "Leader Confesses: Says He Sold Panama Canal Defense Plan to Foreign Nation," *New York Times*, February 27, 1938.
143. Ibid.
144. "Reich Plot to Get U.S. Defense Plans Outlined by Hardy," *New York Times*, October 18, 1938.
145. "Nazi Spy Suspect Set Up Short Wave Station in Hollis," *Brooklyn Eagle*, February 10, 1942.
146. "Long Island Sabotage Try Aired in Trial: Grumman Worker Asked to Obstruct Production," *Newsday*, February 6, 1942.
147. "Girl Nazi Spy Tells of Ludwig Fight, Lucy Boehmler Testifies That 'Write Marion Pon' Meant to Notify Gestapo Head," *New York Times*, February 6, 1942.
148. "Spy Jury Told Code Words for Long Island Air Plants," *Newsday*, February 5, 1942.
149. "Spy Had Secrets of Hawaii Listed: Report Intercepted Here Early in 1941 Told of Information for Yellow Allies," *New York Times*, February 10, 1942.
150. "Girl Spy, 18, Gets 5 Years in Prison," *New York Times*, March 21, 1942.
151. "Sinking of Ships Linked to Spy Ring: Data on Vessels Here Sent by Ludwig to Himmler, Girl Accomplice Testifies," *New York Times*, February 5, 1942.
152. "6 Nazi Spies Guilty in First War Trial: All Face 20 Years," *New York Times*, March 7, 1942.
153. "Blonde Mata Hari Tells of Spy Plot: Toured LI Military and Defense Plants with Nazi Agents," *Nassau Daily Review Star*, February 4, 1942.
154. "Borchardt Tells of Abuse by Nazis: Man on Trial as Spy Says He Spent 16 Days as Prisoner in Dachau Concentration Camp," *New York Times*, February 28, 1942.
155. "Espionage Trial on Today: German Geographer Among 7 Who Will Face Jury," *New York Times*, February 3, 1942.
156. "6 Nazi Spies Guilty."

157. Ibid.
158. "Jail German for His Part in Spy Plots," *Madera Tribune*, October 19, 1946.
159. Christopher Verga, *World War II Long Island: The Homefront in Nassau and Suffolk* (The History Press, 2021), 13.
160. "Engineer Seized as Spy," *Newsday*, June 30, 1941.
161. Verga, *World War II Long Island*, 14.
162. "Spy Trial Hears Adventure Story: South African Described as Veteran," *New York Times*, October 22, 1941.
163. U.S. Department of Justice, Federal Bureau of Investigation, Duquesne Spy Ring Case Write Up, March 12, 1985, declassified, FBI Vault archives, page 1.
164. "Spy Suspect Tells of Dynamite Plot," *New York Times*, October 23, 1941.
165. "Roeder Aided by Jap Agent in Espionage," *Nassau Daily Review-Star*, September 21, 1942.
166. "FBI Shows Movies of Spy Rendezvous: Agents Tell of Hearing from Hiding Place, Plan to Wreck General Electric Plant," *New York Times*, September 18, 1941.
167. "Trailed Two Years: Suspects in Four States Got Defense Secrets, U.S. Chargers," *New York Times*, June 30, 1941.
168. "U.S. Bomb Sight Sold to Germany, Spy Jury Is Told: Former Inspector in Norden Plant Disposed of Data in 1938, Prosecutor Says," *New York Times*, September 9, 1941.
169. Ibid.
170. "Normandie Fire Due to Carelessness," *Newsday*, April 15, 1942.

The Benson House

171. "FBI's Long Island Radio Duped Nazis 4 Days Ago," *Newsday*, September 11, 1941.
172. "Nazis Sought Info on Iceland Here," *Newsday*, September 17, 1941.
173. "Federal Bureau of Investigation Memorandum for Director. Re: Fritz Ernst Rudloff with Aliases Espionage," March 28, 1942, page 5, https://vault.fbi.gov.
174. Raymond Batvinis, *Hoover's Secret War Against Axis Spies: FBI Counterespionage During World War II* (University Press of Kansas, 2014), 189.
175. FBI, "ND-98: Case of the Long Island Double Agent," https://www.fbi.gov.
176. P. Foxworth, Assistant Director, FBI, to Director Hoover, German Orders for Mosquera to Acquire Information on Industrial Manufacturing and Atomic Experiments, May 7, 1942, https://vault.fbi.gov, page 2.
177. Raymond Batvinis, "Long Island Home's Secret Role in WWII Espionage Revealed," NBC 4 New York, June 6, 2014, https://fbistudies.com.

Fighting Misinformation Through Propaganda

178. David Wittels, "Hitler's Short-Wave Rumor Factory," *Saturday Evening Post*, November 21, 1942.

179. War Rumors Manuscripts, Image 9, Administrative Information and Correspondence, World War II, Rumor Project Collection, Library of Congress, https://www.loc.gov/resource/afc1945001.afc1945001_ms01002.
180. Project for the Analysis of Rumors, Administrative Information and Correspondence, World War II, Rumor Project Collection, Library of Congress, January 17, 1942, page 2, https://www.loc.gov/resource/afc1945001.afc1945001_ms01002.
181. War Rumors Manuscripts New York, Image 12, Administrative Information and Correspondence, World War II, Rumor Project Collection, Library of Congress, https://www.loc.gov/resource/afc1945001.afc1945001_ms01002.

Last Gasp of Nazi Intelligence and the Forgotten POW Camps

182. John Strausbaugh, *Victory City: A History of New York and New Yorkers During World War II* (Twelve Press, 2018), 247.
183. Leo Margolin, "Bus Driver Seized as Spy," *PM New York*, September 10, 1942.
184. Ray Blair, "Nassau Man Faces Death as Spy: Accused of Sending News of Planes," *Newsday*, September 10, 1942.
185. "Alien Roundup Takes 3 Here," *Nassau Daily Review-Star*, December 9, 1941.
186. "Valianski Is Seen as Key to Spy Ring: Central Islip Waiter Held for Robbery Admits, He Is Gestapo Agent," *County Review*, April 24, 1941.
187. "Seize 'Nazi Spy' at Camp Upton," *Newsday*, July 1, 1945.
188. "Hart Faces Court Martial as Traitor Trained Spy of Nazis," *Newsday*, December 24, 1945.
189. Jad Abumrad and Robert Krulwich, "Nazi Summer Camp," Radiolab, May 22, 2015, Aliceville Museum, Oral History Project, Aliceville, Alabama.
190. Reiss Matthias, *Controlling Sex in Captivity: POWs and Sexual Desire in the United States* (Bloomsbury, 2018), 32.
191. "Army Reveals the Closing Up of Camp Upton," *Nassau Daily Review-Star*, September 1, 1944.
192. "Report from the Swiss Legation About Camp Upton, Aliens Division," April 3, 1942, Longwood Library, Bayles Local History Room, Camp Upton File.
193. Donald Bayles and Paul Infranco, *The History of Camp Upton: World War I Through World War II*, Longwood Society for Historic Preservation, Middle Island, New York, Letter excerpts from POW Josef Kraft, 2017, 169.
194. Kirk Price, "Vets Turned Down While POWs Work at Upton, Goll Says," *Newsday*, December 6, 1945.
195. "Noble—and Dumb," *Newsday*, July 12, 1945.
196. "Kuhn Departs Today on Way to Germany," *New York Times*, September 15, 1945.
197. "Fritz Kuhn Death in 1951 Revealed, Lawyer Says Former Leader of German-American Bund Succumbed in Munich," *New York Times*, February 2, 1953.

The Shadow of Camp Siegfried

198. Howard Breuer, "Camp Siegfried: Camp History Lingers," *Suffolk County News*, August 7, 1986.
199. Nicholas Casey, "Nazis Past of Long Island Hamlet Persists in a Rule for Home Buyers," *New York Times*, October 19, 2015.
200. Ibid.

ABOUT THE AUTHOR

Christopher Verga is an instructor of Long Island history and Foundations of American History at Suffolk Community College and an instructor in Politics of Terrorism at John Jay College of Criminal Justice. He is a contributor to *Fire Island News* and the online local news sites Greater Babylon, Greater Bay Shore and Greater Patchogue. His published works include *Civil Rights on Long Island* (Images of America), *Bay Shore* (Images of America), *Saving Fire Island from Robert Moses*, *World War II Long Island: The Homefront in Nassau and Suffolk*, *Cold War Long Island* and *The Ferguson Brothers Lynchings on Long Island: A Civil Rights Catalyst*. Christopher has a doctoral degree in education from St. John's University. His dissertation work included studies of Long Island Native Americans and the impact of tribal recognition within their cultural identity.